No End Of The Bed

A Memoir

Lauren J. Barnhart

KNOTTED TREE PRESS

Knotted Tree Press
www.knottedtreepress.com
Seattle, Washington

An excerpt of this book originally appeared in
Jersey Devil Press in slightly different form.

Knotted Tree Press can bring an author to your live event.
For more information or to book an event, please contact us:
info@knottedtreepress.com

Cover Design by Lauren J. Barnhart

Though this is a work of nonfiction, names have been changed
and certain situations and characteristics are composites.

ISBN-13: 978-0615776958
ISBN-10: 0615776957

To Michael
Who taught me to shed the layers until I got to the truth.

No End Of The Bed

George,

Take this book
to bed with you!

"You have to be wiped out as a human being in order to be born again an individual."

Henry Miller

Chapter 1

It was my last attempt at going to church. My palms were pressed together between my knees and I was praying for a way out. Silent seconds of anxiety divided the pastor's booming clichés.

All I could think about were bodily functions. Spittle gathered in a puddle in my mouth and I knew the inevitable swallow would bring on a groan from my stomach. I wanted to flee to the restroom, or be outside in the air where I could feel normal again. Out in the world, drinking coffee and eating an omelet at a cafe with a blanket of voices, music and clattering plates. If I stood up from my grey theater seat now, and walked towards the exit, two thousand faces would turn to watch me leave. So many faces, that they blurred off into the expanse of the massive auditorium. Each one, I imagined, held a different brand of judgment.

Going to church was the only way to avoid the looks of disappointment from my parents. They had done their best to ingrain in me that without Jesus Christ as my personal savior, there is no life, no hope, only death and damnation.

It was all just the opposite for me. As I shook off the hand-me-downs of religion, I felt free for the very first time. I didn't have to hide my personality, censor my creativity, or repress my natural instincts. To be what my family wanted, I would have to deny myself. I'd already spent twenty-two years doing that.

I searched the congregation for handsome men. None of them ever talked to me, or even looked in my direction. It was impossible to tell if they found me attractive, since they were just as timid as I was. The best of them were already married, and breeding like crazy. As soon as one baby popped out, another was on the way.

Pastor Tim pulled my attention back to the podium with an echo of my thoughts, "All of you out there who are married… you're breeding like rabbits! Praise Jesus. You're bringing up beautiful families who will serve the Lord all the days of their lives.

"And for you single men out there, choose a wife wisely. Don't choose a woman for shallow reasons. How does she treat her family? What does she give back to the community? These are the signs of a good woman. A woman who puts others before herself."

I grimaced. This sort of woman sounded like a bore. The term, "Put others before yourself," always rang so false to me. I'd never met a single person who was happy doing that. Instead, I saw resentment towards every ungrateful person they'd sacrificed their life for.

It seemed to me, that if we all just took care of ourselves first and everyone else after, we could all have a go at fulfillment. Society could function at a higher level. There would even be *more* to give, from more time to grow.

I saw all the aging mothers who had let themselves go. Their husbands weren't attracted to them anymore; their kids embarrassed to be seen with them in public. But they'd sacrificed everything. Their aspirations, their vibrancy, even their own health. And if their husbands deserted them, they were too outdated for the work force.

"And you women," he continued, "Uphold yourselves to

2

the highest purity. What is it with thongs these days? Our women are being told by society to objectify themselves. But let me tell you, women. Only whores and prostitutes wear thongs. Don't succumb to societal pressure and fall to that level."

My eyes widened, eyebrows raised. *Thongs?* I looked around. Was anyone else in shock? Had he been living in a cave for the last ten years? Who didn't wear thongs? I thought of the hot pink cotton thong under my form-fitting black pants. A world of protruding panty lines was not a world I wanted to live in.

I pictured all the women around me, throwing their thongs onto the stage with shouts of "Hallelujah!" and "Praise God!" as Pastor Tim kneeled, leaning back with his pelvis jutting forwards. His left palm lifted up to the heavens while the right grasped tightly to his big microphone. His face shown with the Holy Spirit as a rainbow of silk, satin and cotton rained down upon him. At last he was what he really wanted to be – a rock star.

I swallowed, ready to duck out. My thong suddenly needed adjusting. But above all this, a painful boredom overtook me as it always had.

. . .

Two weeks later I woke up next to a random guy I met at Starbucks. His name was Scott. It was the first and last time I ever got involved with someone younger than I am. He seemed mature for his age, but it was hard to tell what was going on with him since he was the silent type.

The night before when I first saw his apartment, I thought it was funny that he had a whole corner set up with pictures and mementos of someone he knew.

"What is this?" I asked, "Some kind of shrine?"

"Yeah. That's my friend that died," he said, nervously scratching an eyebrow.

"I'm sorry."

We sat on the couch and he offered me a glass of wine. He wasn't even twenty-one yet. I didn't ask where he got his supply.

"So I was watching *Real World*," I said, trying to lighten the mood, "and the gay guy on there actually lost his virginity to his babysitter. Isn't that crazy?"

"Me too, actually," Scott replied, solemnly.

"What? Are you serious?"

"Yeah, I am."

I desperately wanted details, but was too embarrassed to ask. More than anything, I wanted to know, who had initiated? I wouldn't put it past him to have been the one to seduce her. Was he ever innocent? I shuttered at the thought that I was old enough to have been Scott's babysitter.

I thought of all the boys I had babysat, who were now in high school or going off to college. When I saw them now, they looked at me awkwardly. Too nervous to say hello, though we had lived through a magical childhood world where they would never hesitate to share their fears, hopes, and dreams.

Scott came over to my parent's house a few days later and charmed them by saying that he could feel the love in the house. They thought he was precious. After they went to bed, we went to the basement and fucked on the carpet. I couldn't relax. The entire time I was sure my dad would wake up and come charging down the stairs, or worse yet, appear at the window to check on us. The sex was awkward. I felt nothing.

A week later, Scott called me. He didn't say much, but as he was about to hang up, he uttered, "Goodbye, Jennifer. I mean, uh, Lauren. I am so digging myself in a hole right now."

"Yeah, you are. But that's okay. I've already met someone else anyway." I hung up the phone before he could say another word.

Chapter 2

Eight months after college, my two cats and I ended up moving into my parent's basement 20 miles northeast of Seattle. I needed to meet new people, and the Internet gave me access to the sort of men I was looking for - worldly, cultured, and mysterious.

As a child, my parents only allowed me to watch the Christian television channel or American Movie Classics. So my taste in men was most informed by Clark Gable, Gene Kelly and Fred Astaire. Throughout my sheltered adolescence I never went on a date or had friends of the opposite sex. I was attracted to effeminate men who were poetic, perfectionist, at ease in the world, fearless and extroverted like an old film star. But there were no boys like that at the schools I went to, and if there were, they would have never noticed someone as quiet as I was.

In a way Irving seemed like a relic from another era. He was twelve years my senior. His online profile read, "My life is rich with experience. I like salsa dancing, good food, delicious wine, and speak Italian fluently." Adding to his aura of romanticism, he asked to meet up at an opera performance in a piano shop downtown.

Traffic was terrible that night and I was late. I rushed in at the last minute with only a brief glance at Irving's face, so that really, my first impression was his shoe. It looked expensive; a rich chestnut brown, polished to a perfect sheen. I liked the way he sat, like an intellectual in a Paris café with his legs crossed. All he needed was a cigarette and a newspaper.

It was a pompous event. Several vocalists sang selections from various operas. Most memorable was a man playing the role of a rooster-like devil, seducing unsuspecting young virgins. After the performance we stood on the sidewalk in the cold night. Lights from the windows were a haze around us as rain drizzled over our black umbrellas down to the pavement.

"Thank you for inviting me out tonight. I've never actually been to see an opera performance before."

Irving gazed at me for a moment. He seemed to be analyzing my posture, the submissive stance of my slightly rounded shoulders. I felt vulnerable, seen in a way so revealing, even worse possibly, than not being seen at all. In defense, I threw my shoulders back and looked him straight in the eye.

"I'd like to take you out for a bite to eat. It's just a few blocks away. I'm hungry, how about you?" he asked.

"That sounds good," I smiled. We walked down the street, cars passing by in an anxious herd of headlights.

"It's slightly unfair of me to take you to the opera when I have the advantage of following the plot. I grew up in Italy, in Florence," he said.

"Really."

"Yes. But Seattle is my home now."

Irving's youth spent in Italy was a part of him, but I saw that taking me to the opera on a first date gave him the satisfaction of being an expert while I sat stupefied. He directed me down a discreet cobble stone alley, past five scooters parked in a corner. The market above was quiet, though a few hours earlier it had been filled with tourists and locals buying fish above the din of buskers struggling to be heard.

He led me into an alcove and reached for the large iron handle of a rustic wooden door. Inside, smoke twisted up through the air as jaded patrons flicked their cigarettes into ashtrays. Paintings caught my eye with washes of deep crimson, midnight blue and umber. Servers lazily stood at the end of the bar looking stoned. We took a seat by the window and ordered two glasses of Pinot Noir. I was drawn into the scene a mile below where a ferry drifted towards Bainbridge Island, its lights creating a glow through the fog.

"You seem a bit more conservative than I am used to," stated Irving.

"How would you know? We've barely talked yet."

"I can just tell." He glanced down at my black leather loafers peaking out from the hem of my tailored slacks.

"People who are too liberal think I'm too conservative, and people who are too conservative think I'm too liberal," I smiled, placing an olive between my lips, delicately nibbling the flesh from the pit. "Irving, it's good to be balanced. I don't believe in extremes of any sort."

The server set the wine down on the table. Irving ordered steak with asparagus and I ordered the risotto.

"I don't believe in moderation. I find wisdom through extremes," he said.

I lifted an eyebrow. "That's what Jim Morrison thought, and look where it got him."

Irving leaned back with his right arm over the back of his chair. He swung his left leg over the right, staring me down. I released my napkin from its fold on the table, and tugged on my too short sleeve. I watched people enter the wooden door and wondered whether Irving's face was too sordid and weathered, or if it spoke of mystery and life experience. I was drawn in by the twinkle in his eye and the subtle twitch to the goatee that framed his luscious lips. All around us were intrusions of words, servers and chairs scraping the floor. Our food arrived, and Irving cut forcefully through his steak, placing it on his tongue. He chewed and set his silverware down.

"Your eyes are very striking."

"Thank you," I wavered.

"Really, very intense." He nestled his chin against his fist, scrutinizing me.

I fidgeted under his gaze, anxiously feeling that my stomach was more full than it was. Pushing bits of risotto to the side of my plate, I turned away and looked out the window towards the harbor. Two barges were docked, waiting to be loaded with cargo. Large vessels made me feel small with their enormity and I held my breath at the thought of drowning, shuddering at the unpredictable, unknowable ocean.

Irving's upper lip twitched and crow's feet crinkled around his dark eyes. "So, how did you lose your virginity?"

"Is that an appropriate question for a first date?" I asked.

"I don't know. Is it?"

"Not really, but I don't care. I was twenty-one."

"Twenty-one?"

"Yeah, believe it or not. It was like the first time I was ever alone in a room with a guy. And all the clothes just came off automatically. I was taught to wait for marriage, but I'm so glad that didn't happen. He was in a famous band and played the trombone; a real class act. I'd never met anyone else like him before. I thought guys like that only existed in my dreams. But much of the fantasy I built up around him didn't really exist. I think he was gay and hadn't come to terms with it yet."

"How did you meet?"

"In a gay nightclub," I replied.

Irving laughed and took a sip of wine.

"Since we're breaking all the rules here, how did you lose *your* virginity?"

"I was preyed upon by an older woman; the mistress of my mother's friend. My mother is an erotic artist."

"Serious?"

"She's most well known for a giant marble penis she named Mr. Cox. The head is dipped in gold and the balls are made for sitting on. She has also done numerous marble vaginas. She even did a series of four to represent the four seasons. She uses the same marble that Michelangelo used. Carrara marble. The best.

"Her friend Lloyd was also an erotic artist. He did paintings and lithographs. He was British, jaded, balding and in his sixties. Nadia lived with him. I'm not sure why she was drawn to him. She looked like Anita Ekberg, right out of *La Dolce Vita* - puckered lips, giant breasts, platinum blonde hair. She was a bit of a fag hag. And she liked to seduce teenaged boys.

"When I was fifteen the four of us were out to dinner and she slowly ran her red high heel shoe up the inside of my leg and began to press the heel into my crotch."

"Goodness!" I exclaimed.

"I was petrified. Sweating with fear. Just when it was too much, she set her heel back on the ground and threw her head back, laughing like a hyena. Everyone turned to stare. Lloyd asked if she was torturing fresh meat again.

"I couldn't take their sense of humor. I was very romantic back then, and I was in love with this young French girl who was my friend, though I had no idea how to break through our innocence and actually make love to her."

"Heartbreaking."

"Nadia kept teasing and played little tricks on me. Two years later when I was seventeen, Lloyd asked me to pose for his interpretation of *St. Theresa of Avila in Ecstasy*. I wore a loincloth and held a wooden stick pointed into the breast of Nadia, obscured by a thick nun's habit and a wimple. But her costume still couldn't disguise her licentiousness. She had the blasé expression of bored masturbation and couldn't grasp the idea of spiritual fervor unless you mixed it with sex.

"The second day in, Lloyd ran out of paint and had to go to the store. Nadia swished over to the window and peered out, watching Lloyd go around the corner. She turned and it seemed that she was moving in slow motion. Her feet appeared one after the other creating arcs of black fabric. She reached up and pulled me down onto the couch, ripped off my loincloth and mounted, riding vigorously until I came. I

9

thought she would suck me up for good and I would be lost forever. I remember this intense fear mixed with pleasure. Then afterwards she said, '*Se lei mi desidera di nuovo, lei sa dove mi trovare.*'"

"What does that mean?"

"If you desire me again, you know where to find me," Irving replied, looking off to the side. "Then instantly, I felt that I had betrayed Lloyd, though they must have had some kind of arrangement. I thought of Celeste, the French girl I'd been pining for; I never got to sleep with her. Nadia grew bored of me very quickly. She only really liked the chase. I started acting up after that. I couldn't take my mother's life. She lives in a fantasy. She couldn't handle me anymore and sent me to Florida to spend my last year of high school at my grandparents."

"That is quite a story. It's so fantastic, I find it hard to believe."

"I know. When I got away from my mother, I had to be the opposite of her. But now I realize, I'm more like her than I initially thought."

"That's kind of beautiful in a way."

I realized then that Irving lived in a complex web of mythology. He feared the ordinary just as much as I did. And he'd only asked me about my virginity so that he could tell his own story in response. I imagined he did this on all of his first dates. But if the story was true, I wondered how his experience with Nadia had affected him. Pleasure mixed with the objectification of his youth. Tossed aside before he could comprehend how quickly innocence grows stale.

Irving pushed back his plate and signed the check. "They have a DJ downstairs. Want to check it out?"

We walked in half circles around tables and chairs and he took my hand as we stepped down the staircase. I tried my best to seem at ease. We reached the dimly lit landing, and he turned and pulled me in close to him. His fingers slid across the small of my back as he kissed me. Awkwardly I tightened my shoulders and hunched up in alarm. I couldn't trust him. He stood back inquisitively. I looked up at him as though caught in headlights; afraid he would disapprove of my reaction. The music was miles away in the silence between us. Disappointed, he gently took my hand and led me down, further into the dark. We navigated the long hallway and without even looking at me he said, "You know, you are beautiful." As though he'd said it a hundred times before.

"You're just saying that. I am not beautiful, and I'm not ugly. Just somewhere in between."

His eyebrows lifted in amusement. Irving kissed me on the cheek and the corners of his goatee bristled against my skin. He was tall and thin with a slight swayback. His dark features were brought out by the sharp angles of his face. Had I ever chosen whom I was drawn to? Men just happened. Each one had consumed my thoughts and emotions, bending my will to their own. In all ways they made me feel insignificant, interchangeable, with a currency comprised only of my body. None of my words ever mattered to them. All they cared about was what I hid below my belt rather than what I hid inside my soul.

Irving and I twirled and laughed in the red-lit room. Distracted by each other, we couldn't quite find the rhythm. My stomach churned as I hoped he would touch me again, and then hoped he wouldn't. It was then that I stopped dancing, brushed my hair from my face, and said, "I should be getting home. It's late."

On the street outside my car he kept touching my face and lingering. I felt overwhelmed by his presence as he circled me like prey. Whichever way I turned, there he was again. All I wanted was to be alone.

Chapter 3

"I need to just be friends with you," my voice wavered through the telephone.

"Okay, I understand. Most women don't last long with me, but one date is quite a record. Usually it takes three," Irving replied.

"I just felt a little uncomfortable with you. Something about you threw me off."

"Like, you tensed up when I kissed you?" he asked.

"But I think you are fascinating. I don't want to lose you altogether."

"I don't want to lose you either."

"Oh good, that makes me feel better."

"You know, I haven't mentioned it yet, but I was divorced two years ago. So I'm at a funny place in my life right now. Not looking for anything serious with anyone. Just dating casually and enjoying my freedom," he said.

"I'm too young to be serious about anyone. If you like someone, you like them. That's all that matters to me. I can't imagine being married."

"I wore her down. After ten years she couldn't keep up

with me anymore." He paused. "I'll tell you what. We'll be friends. I want to entertain you."

"I could use an entertaining friend. Lovers never last."

"Tomorrow night we should go to this crazy circus I heard about, and then to a party my friend is having. We can meet at my house."

. . .

We parked on a deserted naval base next to the water, by a building made up of cement blocks and broken down windows. Irving had convinced me to wear a black furry vest, which felt contrived. To relax my nerves, I kept petting the dark synthetic fur as I admired Irving's black polyester shirt covered with orange flowers. We made our way to the ominous old building.

"Mysterious place to have a circus. It's almost as though it's top secret," I said.

"It is, darling," he teased. I hated terms of endearment and grimaced. Walking into a black room, people milled around drinking wine. Spinning ten feet up in the air, two ample girls contorted their limbs across hoops. Long black hair spun round in wide arcs while fishnets became a blur of black mixed with white skin. For their final move they dropped low into an upside down spread eagle pose. I glanced over at Irving who seemed mesmerized by more than just their flexibility.

"Heavenly," murmured Irving.

"You are so transparent," I said.

"You're not impressed?"

"I am. But I think you're impressed for all the wrong reasons."

"There *are* no wrong reasons. They have marvelous flexibility!"

His steady gaze on their flesh somehow excited me, though I was angry that it did. We sat down and the show began with gothic Victorian musicians tramping about, blowing brass to bawdy tunes. Ghoulish eyeliner and white powder gave the performers an ancient pallor. They had little practice behind them, minus one supremely talented aerialist. Her muscles flexed and gripped ropes thirty feet high, spinning and flipping fearlessly to the campy rhythm of the horn section below. A nineteenth century erotic wrestling match ensued, with two slightly overweight girls going at it, flesh quivering as they knocked each other to the ground. Intermission began and Irving yawned.

"Lauren, I really can't stay for more. Let's get out of here."

"Are you sure?"

"My attention span is running low. Not much for shows."

My feet didn't want to move. I had never seen a show so imaginative and strange.

"Really. We should go get some liquor at my place and then head to the party."

"Okay," I said, swallowing a protest. We left the building, and he feigned to keep me warm by putting his arm around my side. I tried to push him away, though a warm shiver ran down my back.

At the house Irving pulled a bottle of champagne and orange juice from the fridge, "A drink before the party!" He popped the cork, poured two mimosas, and sat on the couch. I stubbornly sat down in the chair facing him.

"Oh come on," he said, patting the cushion beside him.

Buried in the comfort of the vest, I looked out at him from over the top of the collar and squinted my eyes at him, "I thought we were going to the party. This is silly. You'll never know how to keep things simple with me."

His eyes caught the light in a strange way so that he was half obscured by darkness, and half golden. He scratched a sideburn, and then patted the cushion again. I remained staunch. He seemed bent to loosen the tightly wound strings of my life. My curiosity wondered what would happen if I let him.

"Whatever," I said, sitting beside him.

His arms slipped around me, and he snuggled into my

neck. It was like putting on a glove. I realized how tired I was of being alone, and wrapped my arms around him in a sigh of relief. The scent of him filled my nostrils and my body was taken over in a rush of blood, nerves and energy. I nestled in as though he were a warm nest where all my needs could be met. He held my face in his hands and I slid far away from reason. Each moment lost its connection to the next. Irving was leading me up the stairs.

Two candles cast a wicked glow against his body. Eastern strings strummed through speakers. We sat cross-legged, facing each other. He brought in my exhaling breath and I inhaled his exhale, in and out, circulating energy. He placed his hand on my chest feeling the movement of my lungs while my hands drifted across his skin and down his lower back. Slowly we wandered languidly through each other, losing track of which limb belonged to whom. I wove my legs around his and our bodies connected. Slipping into a unified rhythm, we swayed like waves through air. I felt transcendent as white light struck a current behind my closed eyes.

Chapter 4

Growing up, I never really talked to any boys until I slept with one. And by that time, they were no longer really boys - especially since I was twenty-one and I gravitated to older men.

In my senior year of college, there was a speaker at chapel who seemed more suited to Junior High students. He neatly categorized the different stages of a relationship through a ladder analogy. The bottom rung was eye contact. The second rung was conversation. The third rung was holding hands. The further up the rungs you climbed, the more dangerous it became. He told us it was best not to go past the third rung before marriage.

I turned to the girl next to me and said, "I started at the top rung and worked my way down."

She gave a nervous laugh. But I knew plenty of people who followed the ladder rule - my sister for example. She and my brother in-law never kissed until a month before their wedding. She was disappointed that they didn't quite make their goal of waiting. Their friends however, *did*.

The girls and boys I grew up with were taught that sex is

dangerous, taboo, disgusting, perverted, depraved, sinful, dirty. And then one day, they get married and all of a sudden – sex is beautiful. But of course, it isn't. The old perceptions remain ingrained, not only in the mindset, but also in the body. Girlfriend's complained that they didn't enjoy sex with their husbands.

The University had a serious problem with Internet porn in the boy's dorms. There were rumors that they wanted to block sites and moderate web usage. But in my opinion, porn was doing them a favor. If they couldn't express themselves with other live human beings, at least they could simulate the experience in the privacy of their dorm rooms.

The dangers of repression became glaringly obvious one day when a group of girls decided to streak through campus. Every year it was the tradition for guys to streak, and it was always during a public event. The first year it occurred while we were all on the lawn watching 'The Creature From the Black Lagoon' in 3-D. All of a sudden naked guys were streaking past the screen – odd because at first it seemed like part of the movie. The next year they rode their bikes through a festival. And the third year, some girls from the Basketball team decided to do it.

They went streaking through the canyon by the dorms – and strangely enough, guys started chasing them down, driven by mad lust. Something comical and bonding and freeing turned into something frightening. Most of the girls darted down a gravel path, trying to get away. They dove into the bushes to hide, getting scraped by stones and branches. Only one saintly fellow came and offered clothes to get them back to safety.

This all reaffirmed for me my distrust and lack of interest in the guys at my college. I had a long list of issues. To begin with, for every six girls there were only four guys. Overall, they were unattractive, lacking in life experience, introverted with women, hypocritical. Basically, they were a direct reflection of myself, and I did not want to be who I was. Up to that point, I had always been at the hands of environment and religion - ingrained to think the way I thought.

When I was young, my mother always said, "The husband is the leader of the household. What he says goes, and I don't question it."

Thankfully her opinion on this has changed since then, but as a child it shaped my consciousness. A woman is subservient, second-class and submissive. She is always accommodating, never says 'no,' and always has a smile on her face. She never puts herself first. She is on the earth to serve the family and to serve others. A career woman is not feminine. Powerful women are masculine and ugly. Women are unclean and menstruation should never be mentioned because it is an embarrassment. Men can't handle the fact that women have bodily functions. Women are emotional, and men are intelligent. It is demeaning to approach a man – he should always approach you first.

Among many girls at my college there was a celebration of the infantile. My friends sported the same haircuts they'd had since the third grade. They liked to wear t-shirts and sweatshirts with cartoon characters emblazoned on them – most popular being Winnie the Pooh and Mickey Mouse. My roommate insisted on putting up hideous Ann Geddes posters of babies in flowerpots or dressed as pea pods. The girls favored the pastel colors of a baby nursery – pink, lavender, lime green, baby blue. Bedspreads ranged from candy-colored stripes to polka dots. Their binders had pictures of puppies and kittens. And yet, they were adults.

One year I asked all the girls on my floor if they would rather marry for passion and adventure or for comfort and security. Every girl chose comfort and security except for my roommate and I. They went to college to get their M.R.S. degrees and I listened to them complain if they didn't get that 'ring by spring'. Marriage was protection from the outside world. A husband could take care of them, protect them, control their lives and make decisions. By remaining infantile, they would never have to come to terms with the fact that everything they believe doesn't match up with reality. Life, for them, is a construct of someone else's making, and it's a sin to question what you've been told.

Chapter 5

"My candle burns at both ends;
It will not last the night;
But ah, my foes, and oh, my friends –
It gives a lovely light!"

Edna St. Vincent Millay

Irving invited me to go to a party on Friday night. We parked the car in front of a large house overlooking Lake Washington, shrouded by a thick layer of fog. A large middle-aged woman invited us in and there was hardly anyone there, though it was eleven. A few people were asking each other what they did for a living while they grazed on carrots, cheese and nuts. We had just arrived and I couldn't wait to leave.

Downstairs, on the orange shag carpet a dazed DJ spun records next to a bartender cutting limes for cocktails. No one was dancing. They stood in groups of three and four muddling ice in their drinks, glancing nervously across the room whenever anyone entered.

"This party is dead. We might have to leave, but wait right here." Irving let go of my hand and swooped through the room. It seemed he knew everyone, though I realized he knew no one at all. His fingers brushed against arms, he whispered compliments into tickled ears and fluttered his arms like a wizard casting a spell.

I stood alone, invisible and insubstantial. I wasn't sure what to do with the empty feeling in my hands. Everyone looked tired and washed up, as though they had languished in a cubicle for twenty years. But as Irving lavished attention, their eyes were lit from within and his courage was contagious. Within minutes, the room became a swirl of dancing bodies. I was both amazed by his charisma and offended that he had forgotten about me.

As I turned to escape to the bathroom, Irving returned and pulled me by the hand to the center of the crowd that had gathered. Spinning around, he brought me in toward his chest, and then broke loose into a strange mixture of salsa and tango. I tried to follow as he jutted his head like a rooster, spinning this way and that. He furrowed his brow and pursed his lips, snapping his gaze in every direction. It was hard not to laugh.

I could see he didn't care how he looked as long as everyone was watching him. But he also wanted the women to feel beautiful, the men to feel sexual, and the night to seem wide open with possibility. A current of electricity swelled in his wake.

Soon we had lost track of how many rum and cokes we'd had, and the room began to shift. I was lopsided in drunken vertigo when Irving began to kiss everyone in sight. First a woman with big hair and bad shoes, then a bald man in a faux fur coat, a dumpy brunette with tired eyes, a poet with dreadlocks, a golden boy whose eyes captured light, a modish woman in a half black half white dress, an aging pornographer with shaggy hair and a mustache, and a wide-eyed artist with olive skin and a stunning nose. I tried to pretend that this was completely normal.

It was now after midnight. Nighttime creatures were appearing in droves. I decided not to be angry over Irving's universal affection. I'd had so much rum I was convinced it would not be hard to one up him. I flirted with the bald man in faux fur and teasingly whipped him with the long leather straps hanging from my belt. The straps graduated to ping pong paddles from the game room, and the rousing spanking spree spread like a virus. There were not enough paddles to go around so people used what they could; belts, spatulas and towels that came down with loud ass smacks. Inspired by the free flowing rum and coke, the bald man began to gallop around yelling, "Cuba Libre!" as his paddle came down on either side with loud whacks.

I quickly spun off my core, entwined with the man and his girlfriend in a corner of the basement. Bright lights glared down in our faces, and the man's head seemed like a light bulb. The girlfriend was short and fleshy. She was older and I could feel her need to exert dominance over me. I was slow to comprehend when lips like fluffy pillows nestled onto mine. I had never kissed a girl before. My stomach turned; I couldn't wait to go back to the bald man. Her long tongue probed into my mouth, flicking like a lizard. The bald man watched with a gentle smile, waiting for his turn.

Just then Irving appeared with a smirk and a twinkle in his half-moon eyes. I looked at him vaguely and gave a lazy smile. He was familiar, and I was lost among strangers. I wanted to be alone with him - away from the jealousy. I had an obsessive need to feel desired.

"Come with me," he said.

"I want you." I looked up at him. He pursed his lips, and for a brief moment, peered at me as though I was a child. We walked upstairs and went through a tiny doorway, climbing up a narrow stairwell into a pint-size secret room lit dimly by a red bulb. We fell over each other with laughter and dizziness. A few people sat around on cushions watching us. I wrapped my arms around Irving, and our lips met. He rolled over me and his fingers squeezed the outline of my nipple. I held his head to my shoulder and kissed him again.

"Why don't you just go ahead and have sex right here? We don't mind watching," chirped an older woman in the corner. We smiled at her, and then looked at each other. He lurched forward and bit into my neck, then gasped for air. I wrapped my legs around him tighter.

"We're missing the party," he said.

"But the party is right here."

"There is more to be had downstairs. I like seeing you with other people."

I squinted at him, "Only if you stay with me. I just want to be with you."

"Someday you won't."

"But today I do."

Downstairs we danced in a circle with the beautiful blonde boy and two strait-laced girls. As we shared caresses and kissed one another, a girl murmured, "Are you sure this is okay?"

"Does it feel okay?" I asked her, like a seasoned professional. The blonde boy smiled at me. I felt drawn in by his golden radiance. The music thumped through the air and vibrated up through the floor.

As the early morning hours arrived, the crowd began to subtract. The pornographer gave me his card, which simply read, 'Director of Films.' An aging hippy with tumbling grey curls and delicate spectacles pranced around telling stories.

"Man, I was making out with my girl in the backseat of a Manhattan taxi, and the driver's like, "Go for it, why don't you just fuck her right here?" So I was like, "If you insist man!" And that guy got a show, let me tell you!"

Irving appeared with our coats and took me by the arm. We were beyond the point of driving, so Irving dragged me to a car where a couple was waiting to drive us. When we arrived at the house, Irving invited them in and directed them to the backyard. I drifted slowly through the house, struggling to take off my coat and feeling sleepy. Irving meandered down the stairs and flipped open the lid of the hot tub. He stripped down to his underwear and as he reached to remove those as well the couple rushed back through the door and left.

"Irving, what are you doing?" I laughed from up on the deck. I tumbled down the stairs as Irving tossed his underwear and jumped into the tub.

"Come in darling."

I looked over the bamboo, "People will see."

"Nah. They're all asleep."

"You're right." I quickly left my clothes in a pile on the grass, and climbed in clumsily. He kissed me.

"I'm over-heating," I said, trying to prop myself up. The steam was too much and I kept drifting towards the bottom of the tub.

"Are you okay?"

"Sleepy," I said, sliding off the seat again. He got out and brought me a big white terry cloth robe. I was too tired to care about the leftover make-up stains on the collar. I wrapped my arms around his neck and he picked me up and carried me to bed. My head lolled as he laid my limp body down on the soft plum sheets, pulling up the duvet. Getting in, he curled up around me, opening the robe to lay his arm across my bare stomach. I breathed in the smell of chlorine, my head damp against the pillow. I closed my eyes, and fell into drunken sleep.

Hours later, I dreamt I was in a red vintage convertible with several beautiful girls. They were yelling and laughing as we raced over a steep hill. The car flipped forwards, burying our screams into the pavement before the car exploded.

I woke up, my head feeling as wrecked as the car. Lying there, I pretended to be asleep, since it hurt too much to be awake. I contemplated how I felt about kissing a girl. Maybe it had been the wrong girl. Yet the soft on soft had been disarming.

"Wake up, we have to go get the car, and I need some breakfast," prodded Irving.

"Bloody hell, I'm awake. What happened last night?"

"Fun happened. Now get out of bed." He snatched the sheets away from me and I felt exposed. The robe had fallen away and I laid there, naked.

"I was invisible last night. You made me feel like I was nothing," I said.

"You're exaggerating, and you're hung-over."

"Everyone but you paid attention to me. If we're going to date then you need to be aware of my existence when we go out."

He sighed, "You do matter to me. I just can't stay focused on one thing for very long."

"I'm not a thing. I'm a person. There is a difference you know, between not being able to focus, and respecting another person's feelings," I chided.

"That party would have been dead all night if I hadn't done something about it. I made that night happen. Apparently I need to keep you cloistered. I'm just too much for you."

"Or the other way around. But I don't mind. As long as when I'm with you I can have you all to myself. I only want you for the sex anyway," I laughed.

Chapter 6

I turned the key into the lock without a sound, hoping that my parents were no longer drinking coffee and reading the newspaper in the front living room. I stepped quietly in and there they were.

"Why didn't you come home last night?" my mother asked, tight lipped.

"Oh you know, I had a little too much to drink, it was late and I got tired," I said. My mother looked at my father seeking direction.

"Well, she's an adult!" he huffed angrily, shaking his newspaper up to his face.

"You didn't go to church today?" I asked, leveling the playing field.

"We don't go every week. It's nice to rest sometimes," my mom said, fingering the crossword dictionary. I wanted to sit and be close to them, but also wanted to wash the night away.

"I'm going to go take a shower."

"What did you do last night, Lauren?"

"We went to this party at some rich lady's place. There were a lot of interesting people there."

"Well, it's good that you're meeting people."

"Yeah, it was fun," I reiterated, not sure what to say next. I turned and walked downstairs. My head was pounding. The shower burned hot across my aching head, and I let the water run down my body as minutes passed.

I remembered the time I was home from college on a break in my senior year. Boredom had overtaken me, and when a server at the mall gave me his phone number, I called him. That night I drove to Seattle and we had coffee and dessert. He lived on a golf course, in an apartment with a giant fish tank. The exotic fish were hypnotic, and I kept losing myself in their movements, forgetting the need to interact with this stranger on the couch. There was no need for talking. He knelt in front of me and began nuzzling my neck and then kissed my stomach. Someone kept knocking on the door, and he asked me to be quiet and ignore it. He took me to the bedroom, and slid down my pants. Towering over me, it was all over before it even began. And then the next thing I knew he was rocking back and forth saying, "What have I done?"

He disappeared into the bathroom for a while, and then came out saying, "I'm so sorry. I feel so awkward."

"Well, I don't feel that way at all. Everything's fine with me."

"I won't be able to sleep tonight. You don't understand."

I was confused, and angry that he couldn't own up to a little fun. It was pathetic, and I wanted to leave. He walked me to my car and I was home by 3am. I slipped quietly into the basement and mused over his strange reaction. Was he religious? Was he married? I would never know, and never spoke to him again.

He didn't fix my boredom. I felt even more bored than before. I looked back on the night and it seemed no words had been spoken. There had been this unbearable silence mixed with the feeling that he had given as little as possible to get as much as he could take. But what was there to take? It didn't even feel like we'd had sex.

In the morning I sat quietly at the breakfast table with

my parents. My dad cut his pancakes into perfect eighths, and carefully poured syrup across the fractions, making sure not to let a single drop ever hit the plate. He bit his lip with concentration, while my mother solemnly swallowed vitamins, chasing them down with orange juice. No one said a word. As the minutes passed and silence rolled onwards, I realized they were upset.

"Why is everyone so quiet?" I asked.

My dad looked up, "Do you realize how irresponsible it is to go to a stranger's house? And you didn't come home till 3am! My daughter is a slut now!"

"I didn't sleep with him! We were just hanging out."

"Why did you go there?"

"I was bored. It's boring here."

"So boredom is going to cause you to ruin your life forever."

I started to cry, while my mother looked down at her plate silently.

"Get out of my house!" he boomed, pointing down the hallway towards the front door.

"I'm not leaving. I'm not leaving you."

"I don't want to have anything to do with you anymore! You're not the daughter I raised!"

"No. I won't leave. There's no reason for me to. This is my home."

"She doesn't have to leave," my mother said under her breath. She stared down at the table, afraid to look at either of us.

"Get out, Lauren!" he shouted.

"Stop it!" I got up and went to the basement, slammed the door behind me, and cried on the bed.

For the first time I realized that my father's love was conditional. Everything I'd believed about him now seemed false. I thought he was unshakeable, solid, bonded by blood and love with me for life. I wondered if he saw a part of himself in me that he wanted to deny. We barely talked for the next six months.

Chapter 7

My sister is a missionary in Papua New Guinea. She came home on furlough right after I met Irving, because she and her husband were expecting their second daughter in May. My oldest niece was three and had no filter.

On the ferry to Whidbey Island, where they live when they are home, my niece expressed her confusion over gender and race.

"That man has a ponytail!" she yelled, pointing to the construction worker behind us. "Boys don't have ponytails!"

The man smirked at us.

"Well, yes, sometimes they do," my sister replied, embarrassed.

"There's a black man over there!" she said, pointing across the aisle. Thankfully, this time the man was too far away to hear.

"There aren't any black men here!"

"Shhh! Keep it down! Actually, there *are* black people here, we just haven't seen very many. Don't you think it's strange that we're the only white people in the village in Papua New Guinea?" asked her mother.

She didn't quite comprehend this and had already moved on.

My niece and I were dropped off in town for a few hours together that afternoon. At three years old, she looked like Shirley Temple. She had perfect platinum blonde ringlets, tan skin, and giant round blue eyes. I hadn't been the first to inflate her ego. Two girls walked by, smiling at her.

"Hey! They think I'm pretty!"

"Keep it down!" I laughed.

We ate ice cream on a bench in the sun, and I kissed her cheeks that were as round as peaches. We walked down the sidewalk and she held my hand. I was so moved by her presence that I wanted to cry. At the bookstore we learned about Ancient Egypt, and at the music store we shook the fruit shaped maracas. Meandering down to the beach, I slipped on seaweed, and she poked holes in the sand, looking for clams. I caught baby crabs and watched them crawl across her hands as her ringlets blew into my face.

"Auntie Lauren, you don't have a little girl. You need to take me home with you, and I'll be your little girl."

My eyes began to water. "I would love that, but how would that make your mommy feel?"

"She'll be fine! Anyway, she's going to have another baby, and I won't be the baby anymore."

"Everyone will love you exactly the same, and don't you want to be a big girl anyway?"

"No. I want to be the baby!" she exclaimed, as she twirled her dress and went running towards the waves laughing.

When I dropped her off and drove to the ferry I realized I hadn't thought about my own life all day long. She made me forget myself, like in that Lou Reed song, "Perfect Day."

"You made me forget myself. I thought I was someone else. Someone good."

After the baby came, my niece did her best to compete at being a baby. They've been competing with each other ever since in their secret world of sisterhood. Sometimes, it's hard to remember that I had a sister like that once, too. I'm not sure, exactly, who my sister is now, or where I can find her.

She wrote me a letter once that said in Jesus we have a common ground. There were many letters back then, from her and my brother in-law, begging me to keep the faith. They told me how strongly they prayed that I would serve the Lord all the days of my life.

The pastor made my nieces promise the very same thing when they were baptized four years ago. I wonder if they will? Or will they challenge what they've been told to think, and find a different path? The older my nieces get, the more I worry that I will somehow lose them. But I do everything I can, to love and support them.

When my sister and I were kids we used to pack our suitcases, hoist everything up on the swing-set, and pretend it was a train that would take us all over the world. It was her favorite game, her escape from boring suburbia.

The night before her wedding, I couldn't stop crying. As her bridesmaids flitted around, she came into my bedroom to comfort me. It didn't matter what she said, I knew that I was losing her. She'd found her husband and now all they needed was a distant place to be sent to. A year later they were gone. That was sixteen years ago.

Chapter 8

"I had a dream," I said to Irving on the phone. "I dreamt that you were sleeping with everyone. Nothing surprising. But then I was sitting next to my sister on the couch, and I just knew. You'd been with her too. I felt it all over. And then it wasn't just my sister, but also my mother, and pretty much all of womankind. I felt as though they had all betrayed me. I turned against my own sex, and hated all of them. And then I went back to you."

Irving laughed, "You have the strangest dreams."

"It was horrible."

"Well, you know that I can't be monogamous."

"I once had a teacher who always said, 'Can't is not allowed in my class.' I like that. Maybe you are limiting yourself."

"Is that so?"

"It's beautiful to be with one person. You learn new things about them everyday. I was raised to believe that I have something special to offer. But you make me feel I am no different, no better than any other woman you could have."

All the thoughts that had been turning around in my

head wanted to break loose.

"When I was married, the details that I learned about my wife depressed me. There is nothing gained in these details, nothing special in sharing a bathroom. It was a waste of time and effort. I could have been spending all those years with women who still interested me," replied Irving.

"But intimacy is a challenge. The women that interest you today could annoy you tomorrow."

"Exactly, Lauren. On the last bit, you are right. I value my freedom to use the exit. And you shouldn't worry. You *do* stand out from the rest. You are young and fresh with ideals I'd forgotten."

"But I won't be like that forever."

"I was once just like you. If we had met twelve years ago we would have been perfect for each other."

"But then I would have been ten and you would have been twenty-four!"

"I guess you're right. I would have gone to prison for that one!"

"We'll just have to settle with bad timing. Or maybe I am here to remind you of things you've forgotten. Anyway, I kind of find your faults endearing. I like that I can see right through you."

"Wow, a woman who likes me for my faults! I should marry you!"

As soon as the idea burst out of him, there was an embarrassed silence between us.

"You shouldn't say things like that," I said.

"I know. Anyway, I have to get going."

"Right. I'll see you tomorrow then."

I hung up the phone, and looked down at the patterns in the carpet. I couldn't believe he'd said the word, "marry." What was he thinking? As much as I wanted to have him all to myself, there was no way I could take him seriously. He was not someone I could trust. Trust didn't matter much when it came to what we had. So I couldn't figure out why we were both hinting around for something more. I think it was my own ego wanting to win. If I couldn't be number one, then why bother?

I challenged him too much. He would probably break it off with me, but I was hooked. His freedom was addictive, and I forgave his faults because he was giving me the world that I'd been searching for. Nights where the universe could open up and bring the most unexpected constellations. Before Irving, it had all only existed in my head. Outside of that, there was church, conformity, fear, guilt, repression, and judgment.

Chapter 9

In high school I lived in the art room, the only place where I could breathe. I painted portraits of strong women who didn't care what other people thought of them. Their proud faces looked into the distance. I wanted what they had. Their genius minds, trails of lovers, mad talent, fearlessness, irreverence and courage. In class, I never said a word. Just painted for hours.

It was a room full of rejects. Almost all of us were close to being dropouts. I had already failed Pre-Algebra and Geometry, with D's in half of my other classes. The closer we all were to tasting freedom, the harder it was to try and succeed. But we felt safe in that classroom where chaos was allowed. There was paint and charcoal dust on the floor, a plethora of props stacked on precarious shelves, and the teacher was a scatterbrained ex-hippy, as introverted as I was.

Everyone outside of that classroom thought we were losers, recklessly gambling with our expensive private education. Those other students were all too preppy to really understand us, blinded by their beamers and tans and

Abercrombie & Fitch.

When the teacher wasn't looking, the shaggy haired boys next to me showed off their baggies of drugs and told stories about getting into trouble with the cops. I listened quietly. We all shared that same suffocation, the feeling of being trapped in sleepy suburbia and monotony. Somehow our paintbrushes made us feel free for a little while.

For my portfolio I did a study of Georgia O'Keefe, first in pencil, then in oils and finally a clay bust of her head. Shaping the clay made me feel like God. I loved the earthen smell of it, wet and seeping beneath my fingers, forming into the shape of a woman I aspired to be like. My art was a witch's ritual – the continual study of magic and self-actualization. If I could shape the head of Georgia O'Keefe, I could shape my own life. Her head was my practice.

But then, after hours of work, the bust blew up in the kiln. I felt like a loser. It had been so perfect before, and now it was a bunch of crumbly bits. The teacher said I could put it back together with white plaster wrap. But when I finished, her head looked misshapen, and the terra cotta clay of the dessert was now pure chalky ghost-like white. So white you could no longer decipher her features.

In college, I continued to paint in my free time - androgynous rock stars and a seashell sticking straight up in the sand as storm clouds swirled above it. An older exchange student from Taiwan saw what I was doing right away.

"This might look like a landscape, but it's really a self-portrait. You are a fragile shell. But look, you are standing strong in the storm!" she exclaimed.

"Wow. I hadn't realized. But you're right! You are so wise."

"Don't say wise. In my culture, wise means old."

I stopped painting after too many people asked me to paint portraits of their grandchildren or photos of them as a kid. There is no life story on a three-year olds face, nothing to tell through paint. They look better in the photograph, always. One girl refused to pay me. The others barely wanted to pay enough to cover the cost of paint. I got fed up. I wanted to take my art back and keep it for myself. But nothing motivated me the way it had before. It felt stale.

I won an art competition with the seashell painting. It was the first year that they offered art as a major at my small university. But I chose to major in fashion and interior design. The art professor happened to be in the main office when I went to pick up my new schedule.

"Oh, lets see what classes you're taking!" he exclaimed, taking the piece of paper from me. He looked down the column where no art classes were listed. Without a word, he handed it back to me and stormed out of the office. At that point, I didn't really know what anyone could teach me about art. All I knew was that art could only be learned through experience.

Chapter 10

It was obvious that Irving was seeing other women, and I accepted our relationship for what it was. He never came out and said it, but his quips against monogamy, the scent of another woman on his breath, the clues left behind, and the Viagra I found in the medicine cabinet all added up. He said the Viagra was to counteract the side effects of Ecstasy, but I knew there was a reason he turned me down for sex in the morning. He was saving his energy for the next girl. I wondered how many there were. His elusiveness built up the mythology until I imagined all the other women were enormously seductive and cunning, lining up into infinity. It bothered me, but I had my own commitment-phobia to deal with.

I just liked to be alone. On one hand I questioned why no one would commit to me in a relationship, on the other hand, I never gave anyone the chance. I kept myself at a distance, guarding my inner universe from the onslaught of people who would never understand it. The girls I went to school with left their big dreams in the dust and ended up with Christian guys, baking cookies, scrapbooking, and volunteering at the local church. I was scared to death of being trapped in a similar fate. But in the crossover, there were a lot of wolves, and I was perfect prey. Brought up to be a nice young lady who never says no and is always accommodating.

I saw Irving two or three times a week and nothing else was expected of me. I valued my freedom and it was easy to be with him until there were other women around.

We went to a fashion show at a nightclub and I knew it would be prime time for Irving to pick up other women. My nerves were on edge. There would always be competition, and I was beginning to mistrust women entirely. The amateur models pranced down the stage in cheap, scanty outfits, most likely designed by a fashion student. Boxy shapes made out of stiff metallic fabrics, crooked seams, and pudgy hems. Afterwards there was dancing, and Irving introduced me to a few of his friends.

As the floor filled with people, I couldn't turn my back for more than a second. Irving kept dancing off with another girl, speaking who knows what in her ear, weaving around as though he owned the club. His friend Tim danced with me to protect Irving from my interference. He treated me with disdain and condescension, as though I had no right to be with Irving. It was plainly obvious Tim saw me as a brainless distraction and I was foolish to even be there. I felt completely alone. Ignoring my own date so that he could hit on other women was ridiculous, and soon my anger overwhelmed me.

I walked over to Irving as he danced with a grinning blonde, and slammed my hand between them. I cut in front, and started dancing with him as though I hadn't done a thing. At first he had a self-satisfied look on his face. The blonde glared at me and tried dancing up behind him. It was almost pointless. I got bored with the battle and walked off, knowing I would at least go home with him.

At the end of the night I approached Irving. He was absorbed in a brunette.

"Can we go home now?

"Ugh," the girl shot me a look, and pushed Irving back. I had won, as always. Or had I?

Later we sat in his hot tub. I was afraid that he was mad at me, but he didn't mention it at all, and neither did I.

"The most beautiful women in the world are the worst in bed," he said.

"Really? Maybe they are too focused on their looks to be in touch with their inner selves."

"They lie there and just submit. It's like making love to a corpse."

"Well, models are good at taking direction," I replied.

"I was once with an over-weight woman who was absolutely wild, one of the best nights of my life. But I didn't feel drawn in by her. One of those things."

"I read a line in a book once, about a woman having sex with a fat man, and riding him like waves of the ocean. I liked that image. I had a very brief phase with jocks. It was sort of exciting to have them carry me around and just be animalistic. But the thing was, there was never one single interesting conversation, in fact, there wasn't even a full sentence. And I never spent a sober second with any of them."

"Jocks and models should all stick together."

"The key to finding a mate is to first know yourself," I stated.

"Do you know yourself?"

"I'm getting there. How about you?"

"I don't know what would make me content. I think I'd just like to find a sugar mama and quit my job."

"Well, it's certain that I'll never be able to support you."

"You live like a cat. Always lounging around and yawning," he said.

"I'm bored all the time. Waiting for the next interesting thing to happen."

"No. You're an idealist who lives in a world of no meaning."

"I find meaning in being here with *you*," I said with a lilt.

Irving smiled, looking at me as his eyes flickered in the light. "But when you are not here with me, or when this passes, what meaning will you have then? Of course, if you ever sleep with someone else, our relationship will be over. It will be the ending of one thing and the beginning of another. Bittersweet," he said, with a smirk on his face.

"You're such an ass," I said, splashing him with water.

The next morning, the sun streamed through the window past the smiling white Buddha in the corner. The face grinned ceaselessly, and I thought to myself that it must know more than I did about spirituality. I was beginning to feel convinced, that there is no fatherly entity up in the sky. Just energy - all connected, all flowing. People can either create their own reality, or submit to what they've been told.

Lying on my side, I stared at Irving, trying to will him to wake up. But even if he did, he wouldn't give me what I wanted. I often left dissatisfied and angry.

"Irving," I whispered. I ran my hand up along his arm, and nestled myself up against his side. "Irving."

His eyelids fluttered and slowly I inched up on top of him, wrapping my arms up under his. I loved to just lie there feeling his heart beat against mine. Our curves connected comfortably as we breathed in unison, stomachs lifting and deflating. But my intense need for him began to make me feel depressed.

'Just say it,' I thought to myself, 'It's not as hard to say it as you make it seem. Tell him what you want.' But I couldn't. It was inevitable; his fascination would drift onto the body of another woman. A woman who had all the same parts, same longings, same thoughts even. What is it to be a woman if all is interchangeable and replaceable? What could I give that no one else could? I had heard that question in many job interviews, 'What do you have to offer us that no one else has?' I never knew the answer and always tried to fumble my way out of it. I was tired of trying to win Irving over.

I lifted my head from his soft white shoulder and gazed at his face, the long black eyelashes, the way his nostrils flared as he breathed, and the full upturned lips that he'd inherited from his mother. I kissed him and he woke up, responding to me in his daze of dreams.

"I want you so much," I said.

"Not today."

"Why not."

"I'm so tired, and hung over. Really." He kissed me, as though this would calm my nerves. My lungs felt tight with frustration.

"Fine," I said, lying back on my side of the bed. I stared at him drifting back to sleep, peaceful. I gazed for a while at his belly button, and thought of the way it had once connected him to his mother. So strange how we all once absorbed sustenance through a tube to our bellies. I thought of his mother, the woman that Irving seemed to worship, and wondered what it would be like to meet her. What lessons on life could she impart? What could she reveal to help solve the riddle of Irving? She was strong. She was everything that I wanted to become. Would I always feel this weak?

I got up, leaving him in bed. Grabbing his t-shirt up off the floor I spread my arms into it and over my head. I trudged down the stairs, rubbing my fists in my eyes. In the kitchen I poured a glass of water from the fridge and went out the back door, sitting on the stairs of the deck in the glaring sun. Another damn Buddha was staring serenely up at me. It was unbearable, all of this serenity surrounding such disconnected people. A border of ecstatic bamboo framed the yard, and at my feet a fig tree sprouted pubescent green fruit. Vines crept over the lattice reaping pea-size grapes. I laughed over Irving's attempt to create Italy in his backyard, resulting in a bunch of half-ripe plants.

The fire within me lessened to a few smoldering embers. The back door opened, and Irving, naked, looked out. "What are you doing sitting there?"

"Thinking. I like to think rather than do. It keeps me out of trouble."

"Whatever."

The door closed behind him. I heard a clatter of pans and knew he was going to cook breakfast to make up for his inadequacies.

"Damn it! I don't want breakfast. All I want is sex!"

The door banged open. "What is your problem? The neighbors can hear!"

47

"That's never bothered you before. I'm tired of pretending that everything is wonderful. It's all on your terms, your rules, your strategies!" I exclaimed, as I got up and walked past him into the kitchen.

"Do you want eggs or not?" he asked, cracking a yolk into a bowl. He stood there, his penis dangling, holding the bowl up with his eyebrow arched.

"Yes, I'm hungry."

"Then what's the problem? Hey, we should do something fun next weekend. How about kayaking?"

"Sure," I said, smiling for the first time that morning.

"I have them in storage. I'll just need to clean them up and get the equipment together. You know you really are *not* a morning person."

"No. Not so much."

He turned on the gas, and the stove clicked up a flame. The eggs sizzled.

"You're impossible," I said.

"That's just the way I like it. Scrambled okay?"

"No. I like them over easy."

Chapter 11

It was the summer after high school and I somehow convinced two girlfriends to go to an eighteen and over nightclub with me. We had no idea what to wear. But I had been thinking about it for months and had begun compiling clothes that seemed appropriate. I put on some brown shimmery flare pants and a tan knit halter-top. Since all of my other clothes were so modest, I didn't have the right kind of bra to wear underneath, so I went freestyle. The girls approved.

When we got to the city, we walked down the street toward the club feeling insecure. A red convertible full of boys pulled up to the curb beside us. "Hey girls, hop in! Lets go for ride!" they yelled.

"No thank you," we replied politely, when in fact we were scared as hell. The guys seemed pissed off. As they sped away one of them called, "Hey! Cover your tits!"

Suddenly I felt like I was back in Junior High when a boy wrote, "BOOBLESS" on his calculator and showed it to me with silent solemnity. All I wanted to do was cover my chest. Why did boys always have to attack us for our bodies? We never did that to them, at least not to their faces. Maybe they were over-compensating for their own insecurities, like being too embarrassed to change in front of each other after gym class.

We made it to the club - some dump called DV8 that changes names every two years. It was Seafair week so all the sailors were in town. I'd never seen a live sailor before. I didn't realize they still wore the same get-up as in old movies like *Anchors Aweigh*. They perched on bar stools watching girls dance. Their muscles bulged beneath white uniforms with white hats perched on their square buzz-cut heads.

I watched all the girls dance. They looked as though they were, "of the world" – spaced out and wasted. It depressed me completely.

We danced and tried our hardest to alert some form of attention while being afraid of what we might attract at the same time. We were invisible. I felt ugly. The sweat and the lights and the used look of people weighed on me, and all I wanted to do was go home and go to bed. But there was something else taking place that I couldn't quite identify and wouldn't admit to. I wanted to understand the inner-workings of the nightlife. I wanted to conquer it.

We left after an hour and went back to my friend's house. Our clothes strewn across the bed seemed silly now. We felt awake. Alarmingly awake. Sitting on the stone floor we talked till 5am. Everyone at the club was fallen and lost – slaves to sin. We knew that scene wasn't for us. We were above all that.

Chapter 12

"Your skin is so rich! Like the olive oil from my country!"
Nico Brindisi exclaimed, as he bounded over to the purple
wall where shelves overflowed with pots, pans, herbs, and
oils. Grabbing a rustic bottle, he took off the cork and turned
it upside down, pressing his thumb firmly over the opening.

"Taste this," he said, offering his finger to me. As my lips
encircled his thumb, the oil hit my tongue with earthiness. At
first it seemed light, then heavy. It changed flavors and tones,
elusive yet expansive.

"You've never tasted olive oil like this before. I promise."

"It's amazing!"

Nico stood with his chest out, bottle in hand. He wore a
red sari around his thin waist and a black tank top. His arms
were muscular with a dark olive tone, and his hair was a
crazed black swirl on top of his head. Though he was inches
shorter than me, he had a personality that made him seem
much larger.

"It's from my family's farm. We have over one hundred
olive trees."

"Why did you leave Italy?" I asked.

"I never feel free there. I have to hide who I am," he replied, looking sad.

I surveyed pictures on the fridge of women tied in ropes, men kissing in vinyl costumes, corsets, whips, and straps amidst photos of his young nieces. A demure girl with red hair stood against the counter sipping red wine. She glanced at me with amusement. Irving sat at the table; quiet and sober, as Nico dashed from one side of the kitchen to the other; chopping an onion and pouring more wine.

"Nico, you must show Lauren your bedroom. I think she would appreciate it," suggested Irving.

"Yes, I must! You are right." He replied. As he grabbed my hand, I couldn't help laughing over his intensity.

We tumbled down the stairs and he swung open the door. The walls were red and towering with vaulted ceilings. My eyes landed on a large velvet swing. "Oh ho ho!" I skipped over, and sat down, pumping my legs and swinging. "Is it safe?" I asked in afterthought.

"It's secured from a beam. I use it for sex therapy. It's the most comfortable position for women that have been abused. They have all the control."

"Fascinating!" I got up and looked out the back window. An old red eight-paned window hung from the maple tree. Each pane housed red stick figures in different configurations. He walked up behind me.

"I dreamt of every type of relationship," he said, "A woman and a man, two men, two women, a couple with a child, a man and child, and a woman with a child. I saw them all and knew that I would never be in any of these relationships. I am the lone person in the middle."

The window swung from the tree, the overcast sky and wind making it appear vulnerable to the elements. I felt a wave of sadness.

"See that old toilet with the rosemary growing out of it? I had a party and some jackass tried to pee in my plants. I cook with those! So you know what I did?"

"What?" I asked, laughing.

"I stomped out there and gave him the boot right in the

ass. He went flying out into the grass. I kicked him out after that."

"Some people are so stupid!"

"Lets go up, I just heard more people arrive. I never know who will show up ever."

"Doesn't that bother you?" I asked.

"Sometimes. But my house is always open."

I stood looking at Nico, half intimidated by his charisma, and half drawn to his warmth. As we left the room, I took note of the boas and whips hanging from the door. I felt a rush, not knowing if I could trust my surroundings, or the people within them.

Introductions were made upstairs. I sat quietly next to Irving, feeling too soft and too young. Women in braids and loud colors sat around the living room. A few jovial, bearded men sat on the floor. Everyone, regardless of gender was freely affectionate with each other. Dinner was ready, and people began to quiet down as they ate. But Nico rarely ever ate, preferring instead to buzz around his guests.

"Wait! Wait! I have a joke!" He turned around and adjusted his nether regions. Facing everyone, he lifted his sarong and exclaimed, "Look! I'm a woman!" Everyone laughed or choked on their food at the sight of him holding his penis and scrotum between his legs to reveal only a perfect V.

"Nico, we're eating."

"Food and sex are the only things I live for." He turned and surveyed the room, "You know, the only things in this house that I paid for were my cooking tools. Everything else was given to me or I traded for."

At times Nico seemed like a child in his simplicity, but then he would offer a profound thought. Many adopted his concepts as their own. I turned and watched Irving eye a girl, afraid of what he might do, or say, or be. Conversations began to breed and journey into different directions.

"So Irving, what do you consider Lauren to be to you?" asked Nico.

"She's my girlfriend," Irving replied.

I looked over at him in shock. "What does that mean?" I

asked.

"Well, what else would I call you?"

"I don't know. Your lover or your friend?"

"Irving, is that fair to call Lauren your girlfriend when we all know the truth?"

"My thoughts exactly," I agreed, frowning at Irving.

"Everyone up!" Nico shouted abruptly. Startled guests looked up from their empty plates. "I want you all to go into my bedroom and lie down anywhere you like."

"What's this about? Some kind of experiment?"

"Orgy time?"

"Just come on," he said, ignoring the questions.

Slowly we all drifted down. Lying on the bed and the floor, guests felt the tingle of anticipation. Irving laid next to me, sharing a smile before resting his head.

"Close your eyes," said Nico, his voice distant and hushed, "And open your mouths." He was in the room now.

"I don't want to know," said the burly man in back.

"Hey man, I'm straight," said another man.

"Since when."

And then there was silence, and the murmur of an, "mmmm." I heard the sound of rustling fabric and sensed Nico was coming closer. Then he was above me, hovering. Dark chocolate ganache oozed onto my tongue. Nico pranced about squeezing the tube into open mouth after open mouth.

"Lauren! It's your turn. You are our sacrificial virgin. You must feed them the second course!"

"Oh my!" I followed him up where he handed me a plate of mango cheesecake bites.

"Don't worry, you'll love this."

I marched bravely to my mission, and entered the room. "Everyone, open!" I called. All around me bodies of all shapes and sizes were lying prone and vulnerable with their mouths gaping open. It took effort not to laugh and spoil their trust. A strange sense of power overcame me as I crouched and placed a piece on the first man's tongue. His lips closed over it as a wave of contentment crossed his face. He maneuvered the cheesecake across his tongue to let it fully wash over his taste buds. Next there was a woman who gasped in delight. I relaxed and watched the anticipation turn into enjoyment. When I finished my round, the guests began to sit up and chat. I returned the plate upstairs where Nico was cleaning.

"Thank you for that."

"Oh nothing. I see that you like to watch. But you need to live, Lauren."

"You know, I have this friend. We were on a student trip in Europe and I hadn't connected with anyone. They thought I was strange for having opinions. For instance, at the Vatican, everyone was kissing the foot of the statue of Saint Peter. It was strange to see the religious emotion. His foot was so worn down, just a stump left really. I heard they'd already replaced it before. Chiseled away by hundreds of kisses," I paused. "Anyway, by the time we arrived in Salzburg, I was feeling very alone. We went to dinner at some traditional place. Everyone ordered Wiener schnitzel with lemon and currant sauce. This girl Donna took one bite of it and started crying out of ecstasy. I fell in love with her right then and there. It was one of the most beautiful things I've ever seen."

"Wow. Where is this girl?"

"Portland."

"Shit."

"So then after that we went to the Mirabelle gardens and got ridiculous. We rolled down a hill like we were little kids, kissed statues, sang, told each other stories. It was so romantic to find a kindred spirit. Why doesn't that ever happen when I'm with a guy?"

Nico turned from the sink drying his hands on a dishtowel, "Guys are afraid to be vulnerable. They care too much what you think."

"Do you think Irving has feelings for me?"

"You tell me. If he does, you would know."

"You're right," I said looking down.

"Never trust a man until he gives you reason too," Nico shook his finger.

"I trust people right away, until they give me reason to not. I must be blind."

"I trust no one, and love everyone. I am an ethical slut!"
I laughed, "I love your honesty."

"But I am lonely. I will never be able to be monogamous."

We returned to join the group downstairs, where some were getting up to leave. I sat on the swing, and Colin began to push me back and forth. I looked up and realized I was the only woman left.

"It's wonderful to watch you swing," spoke the burly man in the corner. Irving sat on the bed with a twisted smile on his face. There was an odd silence in the red room, as though the circus had just left town.

"It makes me dizzy. I must be getting old."

"Hardly darling. You are always the youngest person in the room," said Irving.

The burly man looked up, "Why didn't Barbara stay? She obviously must not be that into me if she prefers going home to work rather than spending time with me."

"So it's okay for a man to put his work first, but not for a woman?" I challenged.

"Well, I never put work first. I just use it to pay the bills," the man responded. A brief silence entailed, as I kept swinging.

Nico affirmed, "I've risen above many things! Except for women." He was silent for a moment. "Maybe I should try being celibate."

"That would never work," I surmised.

"What do you mean? Of course I could do it. I dream of letting it all go."

"Not on your life," said the burly man.

"One hundred women would be broken hearted," Irving proclaimed, sweeping his arm into the distance.

"In the village I was born in, I was next in line to be the priest. But my mother knew better, so instead of giving me a religious name she called me Nico. The man who took my place, I ran into him once in Seattle. What he was doing here, I don't know, cause I pretended not to see him."

"Why?" I asked.

Nico spun around and flailed his arms, "Cause I was

fucking wearing a dress man! What's he going to do? Go back and tell everyone I'm a fag? My family wouldn't understand."

"So Nico, what are you then?" asked Irving.

"I'm a lesbian. I love women, but sometimes I sleep with men. Never emotionally, just sexually."

Irving looked up. "People think that I'm flamboyant, but I have no desire to be with a man."

"Good to know," I replied.

Irving stood up, "Lauren, I'm getting tired. We should go."

"Okay."

"He's a lucky bastard," said Nico, pointing his thumb towards Irving.

"Then why doesn't he show it?" I asked, shrugging my shoulders.

"Well, at least he's honest with you," Nico replied.

"He's only half honest," I replied. "He prefers mystery to telling it like it is."

Irving laughed knowingly. I rushed to give Nico a hug and felt myself sink into his warmth. He burst out in emotion, "Oh please! You must go. Don't make me want you so much!"

I laughed him off, but I never wanted to let go.

Later on, in the darkness of Irving's bedroom, I turned my back to him and spooned against his warmth.

"I could see having a child with you," he said into my ear.

"Are you serious?"

"Well. I *am* rather drawn to your DNA."

"Ha!"

"But you know, if it ever happens, we could have joint custody. I don't think I will ever marry again."

"That is somehow, outside the realm of my imagination, though I would be honored to have your child, if it were to happen."

"Really?"

"Of course."

He kissed the back of my neck and was quickly drawn into my body. But it did not feel the way it had felt in the beginning. It felt like an empty series of motions. I wove my hips around him, and the more I gave, the more his body tightened and traveled far away from me.

I felt helpless with no response beneath my fingers. I realized he was afraid of all that he wanted. A longing for something beyond our grasp slipped through our fingers and fell to the floor. Running my hands along his skin, his face looked contorted and strange in the dark. I looked into his eyes, waiting to feel his presence and wondered what I could do to become more interesting, more sexual, and more alive to him. But in reality, I knew it would never be enough. The thought of being so easily replaced made me feel like a failure.

Exhausted we slept at two opposite ends of the bed, and in the morning readied for the day in bathrooms at two opposite ends of the house. I left as he was going to work, and stopped to have a coffee and Danish. Sparrows ate crumbs off the table, and I smiled at their simplicity. I observed that adults never noticed the birds. They quickly rushed by, blind to their surroundings. Only the children noticed. Pointing and laughing, alive and alert, they were open to the full range of life, unafraid and whimsical.

Chapter 13

"People will believe anything.
Except, it seems, the truth."

Jeanette Winterson

Growing up, my mother's entire social life was within the faith. Besides church on Sunday, she attended Wednesday night services, ran a Senior Citizen's Bible study the next morning, and went to Praise night at Mrs. McMaster's house on Friday night's. But her Women's Aglow meetings really took the cake. They met up once a month in various banquet halls. The only man I ever saw there was a handsome African American pastor. Everyone was in love with him. At the time, I was about six years old, and he told me that he liked the dress my mother had forced me to wear. I felt ridiculous in frilly things with bows and petticoats. But the tights were an even worse torture. I couldn't stop scratching my legs.

At these meetings the energy would reach a frenzy, building to a climax until around twenty women would go up front. Amidst howling and shrieking and blubbering sobs, the pastor would shout, "By the power of Jesus' blood you are slain in the spirit!"

Instantly they would all fall, flat on their backs. It was very funny to watch. It wasn't as though they would sit on their asses and then fall back. It was more of a complete backwards faint. A long row of over-weight women in potato sack dresses just lying there, some of them passed out, others speaking in tongues.

One time a woman came with a neck brace claiming it was a permanent injury. The pastor laid his hands on her, along with five women praying out loud in a din of nonsense. Eventually the woman couldn't take it anymore. She busted off her brace and started yelling that she'd been healed. Women's Aglow was always good for a show.

There were other meetings like this one. One night we went to see a traveling evangelist who was a faith healer. Two parents brought in their screaming three year-old and told us he was possessed by a demon. It seemed to me he was just tired or sick or maybe had a psychological problem. But the pastor started yelling, "Release him from this torture! Set this boy free! In Jesus name!"

The boy screamed even louder. I had to admit, it was eerie. And it went on and on, until finally the boy stopped crying, and they walked off the stage. Yes, the stage. Everything seemed staged. Like theater, like an over-abundance of emotions, like hypnotism. The pastors all used that same rhythm in their voices, as though they were all from the south. It lulled you into believing what they said.

"You are getting very sleepy," pause, "When I count to three you will close your eyes. One... two... three," pause, "I will use the Bible as mind control. And because of the all-knowing tone of my voice you will never question me, I will use the pulpit to be high above you, and the words that I say will be the words of God. I will be like God to you. I will comfort you, but I will also fill you with fear. Because you would not want to falter in front of God, just as you will be your best for me. And you will give me your devotion, your money, your life, and your will. As a congregation you will grow, and feed my ego. And we will grow in strength. We will take over the world in our spiritual revival. We will spread to the far reaches. And I will be your leader. I will be your father. When I count to three you will be free from your own weakness, and will understand the strength in being my flock. One... two... three!"

My mother wouldn't question the pastor, or the Republican president, because she was told their words were the word of God.

Throughout childhood I went through an inner battle that no one else could see. Pretending to be good was so stifling. At four years old, in church singing hymns, I thought it would be funny if I sang in potty talk instead. No one could hear me. But I felt liberated from all the staunch repression, free as I could be in my pee-pees and pooh-poohs and on and on in my own personal mantra. The boredom of the following sermon never mattered after that. I had committed my first act of rebellion against being made to sing words I did not feel.

I was sixteen and my mother and sister took me on a women's retreat. Maybe I could finally prove that I wasn't a failure at being a Christian. They asked if anyone would like to come up to receive prayer. I went up and asked to receive my prayer language. Three women laid hands on me. I closed my eyes hard in concentration, desperately wanting to feel something. Their touch sent a chill down my back. I looked over to the right and could see my mother prostrate on the ground through the crowd. Turning back, I zeroed in on my attempt to feel the presence of God. But there was nothing. Only my own mind telling me that now would be a good time to begin speaking gibberish.

When I opened my eyes, everyone was so happy for me. I had grown in maturity as a Christian. Their hope in my future was replenished.

Chapter 14

It was the morning of the annual Summer Solstice
Parade in Fremont. Every year one hundred nude, painted
cyclists rode through the streets beckoning the parade
onwards. A kaleidoscope of people painted silver, periwinkle,
cotton-candy pink, orange, purple and blue; tree people,
rainbow people, super heroes all passing by in an array of
shapes, ages, sizes; bulbous or pointy, stubby or dangling.
Even a few naked roller skaters joined the cyclists, swirling to
the beat of the music. Thousands gathered, cheering down the
three-mile stretch, while two somber faces on the main corner
held fiery signs that read, "You're All Going To Hell."

I stood on the sidewalk, watching the nudies pass by with
a friend from high school. Celebrating a pagan holiday, I'm
certain, was not something she'd ever envisioned doing,
although, all holidays were originally pagan.

At last I saw Irving and Nico making their way down the
street. Nico chose to go as the bride of the sun. In white paint
with red hearts, he wore a flimsy veil, which added drama to
his sharp, masculine movements. He had found a dilapidated
bike that he painted white and wrapped with garlands of

flowers and tulle. Irving hadn't been sure what to do. Post-spray, he looked like a strange sort of blue Puck with a devilish face.

A cast of colorful characters peddled in their wake - a blubbery bumblebee whose sagging breasts looked charming beneath yellow paint, a silver angel whose body became a series of reflective angles shining in the light, a green man whose painted beard looked like fuzzy moss, and a flowery man who had painted everything but his penis.

"Irving! Nico!" I called.

They waved and rode their bikes over to us. An older couple next to us was surprised that I actually knew the crazies in the parade. My friend laughed nervously, as Irving and Nico came to a stop and kissed my cheeks.

Irving lifted his penis for me to see, "Look I painted a red smiley face on it!"

"Wow, that is something."

Nico glanced at the couple next to us, "Are these your parents?"

"Oh no! Of course not!"

"Wouldn't that be great, if this was how we finally met them?" asked Irving.

"They would never forget it."

"We have to keep rolling, see you soon, Lauren."

Nico sped away with no hands, his white backside flexing as he pedaled. Irving zigzagged back and forth, looking back with a grin on his face. Further down, the two held hands as they rode down the center of the street. Colorful people drifted by like paintings past the onlookers – tourists, neighbors, parents using strollers as weapons to get by, frat boys chugging beers. The cops stood guard looking on in amusement, giving the civilians a hall pass to bear their genitals and drink booze on the street.

Giant puppets, aging hippies, and a few token drag queens appeared. Belly dancers shimmied their shake in silver coins and chiffon - a few dancers short of being a billion belly march. Samba drums brought up the energy with sequined beauties shaking their tail feathers. The fertility float passed by surrounded by dancing birth control pills and sperm, topped with a pregnant Venus. Creature people loped around on stilts and the crowds swelled along the sidewalks. There were no formations, no straight lines. The parade pressed on in a jumble of swerving and whirling.

Ending at Gas Works Park, people lounged on the grassy hill, lazily looking out over the water and the city beyond it. Irving and Nico had already left. I admired a beautiful girl with only a hat on, playing the guitar. My friend commented that it just wasn't safe to put yourself out there like that. But secretly I wished that I could feel that free.

Chapter 15

Two months prior, I spent the weekend in Portland to see my friend Sonja perform in *A Midsummer Night's Dream*. She was one year younger and in her senior year at our small Christian college. I would be attending the show with Kayla, who was my age, married, and obsessed with wearing too much make-up. They were both physically stunning - Sonja looked like a romantic poet from the twenties with a perfect black bob, and Kayla had intense Northern Italian features with large blue eyes, luscious lips and blonde hair.

The three of us shared a passion for literature and fashion. In my last months of college, we religiously sat in the courtyard of the coffee shop, drinking too many super sweet mint iced mochas (also known as Grasshoppers). We gossiped over our classmates and discussed what books we wanted to read. I had met Kayla in my Modern Novel class, and Sonja lived on my floor sophomore year. We had a bond stronger than I had experienced before. I looked forward to the moments I could share with them each day, and I loved them intensely.

After I graduated, I spent a May term doing

photography, and reveled in turning Sonja into a glamour queen. I put her in my party dresses and took photos of her that resembled old Hollywood stills. I did a photo shoot with Kayla at the Quaker Cemetery, where she posed on gravestones, too beautiful and irreverent to care about death. Every day with them was like a party, and I was certain the party would never end.

That day in April, Kayla and Sonja and I were to meet up at a restaurant for lunch. Sonja was late. Since Kayla was married, it felt safe to talk to her about sex, and I had no one else to talk to. I was giddy, and bubbled over with my latest details. It seemed important to debunk all of the lies that I had been told before. I wanted everyone to feel as liberated as I did.

Kayla laughed over my stories about Irving. She shared her frustrations over her husband, who always seemed distant and emotionally unavailable, kind of like her father.

I had spent my entire life being repressed with my lips zipped shut. So to make up for it, I now had to let everything loose. For those who were in my path, it was like a tornado of emotions and raw sexuality that came flying out. Not only did I write down every little experience, I needed to talk to people too.

Sonja arrived, and being an idealist, she asked the typical questions. "Has Irving met your parents?"

"No, that's not important. It's not that kind of relationship."

"Could you see yourself marrying him?"

"Definitely not! Really. I'm learning so much and having fun. The sex is ridiculous!"

Sonja grimaced. She couldn't understand. She had just gotten over a two-year crush on a guy who didn't even know she had feelings for him. And now she was swooning over a fellow actor who played Oberon in the play. Neither of them knew she existed.

"Well, I think you're selling yourself short," she said.

"I'm not selling anything. I'm bathing in the experience of life!"

Sonja left to get ready for the play, and later on Kayla and I enjoyed watching her onstage. I didn't know it would be the last time I would ever see them. After a few weeks, I gave up on calling Sonja because we were not as close. But with Kayla, I couldn't believe it. I continued calling her several times a week for the next two months. Each time I got the answering machine, I had the distinct feeling that she was in the room listening to my voice. I was like a spurned lover, incredulous that she could cut me off.

I had a friend, Richard, from the neighborhood by our college, who religiously sat at the coffee shop with his English Mastiff. Richard was tall with a massive broad chest and hair down to his waist. His dog looked like the guard of a medieval castle. Both were quite imposing, though underneath, sensitive teddy bears. Being the good friend that he was, he talked to Kayla one day, and broke through the small talk with, "So, have you talked to Lauren lately?"

"No, not in a while. Have you?"

"Oh, we had a falling out," he lied.

"Yeah, I stopped answering her phone calls. She's just not Christian enough anymore. She changes with every guy she meets," Kayla said.

There was satisfaction in hearing the truth. Every friend I ever lost, I lost due to religion. It's the idealism, and the need to feel protected and safe. Life seemed too short to live in the comfort zone.

Chapter 16

I entered Irving's front door and kissed him. His mouth had that salty sea taste of a woman. I looked into his eyes, which had a mischievous cast, and felt as I often did, that he was thinking of someone else. I praised myself for not being in denial amidst pangs at my failure for not capturing him completely. I hated the way Irving's eyes often drifted over my head to catch a glimpse of a woman behind me. And though every moment I spent with him was glued into my consciousness, he remembered so little of it.

"Can we sit outside for a minute? Would you like some ice water?" he asked.

"Sure."

He pressed two glasses one after the other into the ice shoot, followed with spurting water. We sat across from each other on the deck, where the sun glared angrily into my eyes. I squinted and looked down. Irving sat complacently across from me. His head blocked out the sun, turning his face into a dark shadow with light suffusing round the circumference of his head. He crossed his legs and tried to appear nonchalant, but his stiff upper body gave him away. One arm rested uncomfortably on the steel armrest.

"Darling, I have to end this," he said.

I tightened. I had spent all the empty hours of my day imagining how this night would play out. This was the last thing I had expected.

"Sure, I could become the good man who settles down with you, have the picket fence and five kids. But ten percent of me would like to be with you, and there are nine other Irving's who want to run around and do their own thing. Lately, I've been feeling like I'm suffocating. And I know you're not happy anymore. I don't know if you ever were."

I couldn't speak at all. My face felt as though it was falling downwards, and the sun was unbearable. Irving had shifted in his chair, no longer blocking the ball of light. The glare emanated, and the tension burned through me. I was sweating. A picket fence! Since when did I ever want a picket fence and five kids? And it seemed to me that he was the one with the picket fence, right outside the front of his house!

"You are too charming a person to be hurt by me over and over. What we have together is a dream and it could never quite be a reality," he added.

We sat there shifting in the uncomfortable metal weaves of the chairs. Minutes seemed to slip past without a sound from me. I looked at the plant, the door, the smiling contented Buddha who now seemed to be mocking me. Then I stared at Irving's knee.

"Well, do you have anything to say to this?" he asked.

"I can't let go of you Irving. I love you too much." Sobs rushed out, releasing all the breath that I had held in. Irving said nothing. He walked casually into the house to get a tissue, as though this was a regular occurrence that he had grown accustomed to. I sat staring at my perfectly creased dove gray pants. A big black mascara-laced teardrop landed right on my knee. It grew like cancer.

Irving came back out and dabbed at my tears and then my pants with a concerned look. He tried to hold me, but he felt like an intruder. I pushed him away and retreated into myself, no longer allowing him to fit against my limbs.

Slumped over and curled in.

"I'm trying to think of something to say that will make you laugh," he said.

"I don't want a fucking picket fence. And I will *never* settle down. You don't even know me."

"Lauren. You're so young. You don't know what you want yet."

"I want you. I want excitement. I want passion. And that's it. You only see what I come from. Not who I am."

"Lauren you know this isn't working."

"Yes. I don't like to share you. It is *my* problem, not yours. I am everything one man needs."

"I agree."

I looked up at him and wiped my eyes.

"I can't hurt you anymore. I don't want you to feel as jaded as I am"

"You don't know how beautiful you are," I replied, "I don't think you even see in yourself, what I see in you."

"How about I take you out for steak? I don't want this entire night to be one big loss."

A half an hour later we sat in a booth at the Queen City Grill in Belltown. "You know, you are the only woman I know that can actually make me feel like a man."

"Really?"

"I often feel more feminine than the women I'm with. You're so elegant."

"I don't think so. But I guess I would like to be like those very elegant women that light up a room when they enter. They make people feel happy."

"It's intimidating."

"Why?"

"I don't know. I'm never sure what to do with you," he said, shaking his head.

"Well. Now you've decided," I stated.

"But we should be friends. Excuse me a second," Irving said, as he slid out of the booth. He walked down the hall to the restroom while I sat alone, cutting my steak with a knife, listening to Frank Sinatra sing, "I've Got You Under My

Skin."

I had expected this, just not today. How did I get here? I mused over his faults. I had ignored them simply because he made me feel more alive than before. I was addicted to the rush of not knowing what he would do next. He slid back into the booth across from me.

"You know, you should meet my mother. You'd love her," he said brightly.

"Where did that come from?"

"I don't know. I could just see you two hitting it off."

"Don't you think that's kind of a funny thing to say right now?"

"Well, now that we're not dating, it's okay. It wouldn't have the same connotations."

"I see."

Later that night, we wanted each other even more than before. We kissed and seemed to be losing our balance. Standing there in the living room, I was hesitant. I walked toward the door, wanting to feel strong rather than give in. He didn't really want me anymore.

Driving home I was wide-awake. I knew that the others could not mean more to him than I did. Within me I felt a world of riches waiting to be discovered. I was taught this, waiting for this, wondering when someone would see so far within me, that no one else would matter in the same way.

It was difficult to grasp onto who I was without Irving. I was a different sort of person when I met him. He had introduced me to a world that exposed a hidden side of my identity. But how could I express that without him? There was no one else in my life that could understand. There was no other place that I knew of, to feel complete openness and freedom. I was returning to silence. I could see that without him, I would be afraid of my own words again. But all I wanted to do was scream.

The next day at dinnertime, I sat down on the deck with my parents. We ate Mandarin Chicken Salad and drank white wine. The birds chirped in the forest and we felt like we were in paradise. I told them what happened the night before.

"Well, I truly respect some of the things Irving had to say to you," my dad said. "The melodrama of your relationship with him is so wonderfully Italian!" He lifted a forkful of lettuce to his mouth and then continued, "You know, before your mother and I were married, the pastor told us, "The truly amazing thing is that you will love your partner more and more each day." And you know what? He was right! It's true!" his eyes filled with excitement and his hands flew through the air.

He turned to me, "Look how blessed you are! You are sitting here on a beautiful day, drinking wine and talking to your mother. You know, I wonder what I would have been like if I had had a mother," he pondered. His mother died when he was three years old. "Probably a little easier to live with," he surmised.

"Don't worry, dad. You're perfectly easy to live with."

"But I would have been more compassionate," he said, taking my hand. For a brief moment, I forgot that pain existed.

Chapter 17

In my junior year of college, I was on the dance team. We were actually not allowed to call it a dance team, and the official term was drill team. Student-run with plenty of drama, and I couldn't stand the other girls. The beauty of the drill team was that it attracted the worldliest girls on campus, and I was intrigued. By the end of the semester we all had our navels pierced. And I was shocked when they started talking about getting boob jobs. Where did these girls come from? Public school?

Claire, who had appointed herself as choreographer, got a few of us together to go to a club in Portland. She invited some guys to go with us. I was in the back of someone's car and all I could see through the fog was Claire driving and laughing hysterically like a maniac. I had a feeling tonight was my night.

For the introverted dancer, the beauty of a nightclub is that your body does all the talking and you never have to open your mouth. It wasn't long before the first random stranger was sidling up behind me and I was experiencing a full body caress for the first time in my life. I wanted more. I danced with a second, then a third, then a fourth, then a fifth. No one else from college danced with anyone. I knew they were probably thinking that I was a whore. I could tell, at least, that Claire was jealous.

"I can't believe you let those guys dance with you like that. What were you thinking?" she asked later.

What's wrong with letting go of our mind's that think too much? Why is it wrong to feel so alive, so good? So different from the ghost I felt myself becoming on campus, where I went months without ever being touched by anyone. Not even a hug.

I repented for my sins the next week in chapel. But the experience made me think that I wanted to be single forever. That maybe a ring by spring was over-rated, especially with the lack of options at our college. I didn't want an M.R.S. degree. I wanted to live. And I couldn't wait to turn twenty-one.

Chapter 18

Irving was roasting salmon on the grill. He had placed the filets on foil with slices of lemon and olive oil. Smoke rushed up to his face as he opened the stainless steel lid.

"Almost done? I'm hungry," I said, standing behind him.

"It'll be just a bit."

"I feel nervous around all of these new people. I don't know why."

"Don't be."

"I just feel so young. Everyone I know is much older and so sure of themselves."

Irving flipped the foil with tongs, seeming twitchy. He fingered something in his pocket, and I figured it was some other girl's phone number.

"Well, the food is almost done."

"Smells good. I just don't know what to say to anyone, you know? Nico and Antonella are speaking in Italian, and Miriam and George are so busy making up for lost time. The only place I fit is with you."

"I wouldn't have invited you if I had known you would be so uncomfortable."

79

"It's not that. I didn't mean that. Everyone is fascinating. I just feel shy right now. Maybe a little intimidated. I want to talk more with Nico, but he's so larger than life. I feel like a dim bulb sitting next to him."

"You'll get over it," said Irving. He pulled the foil onto a pan, and turned off the grill. "You will love him. I promise."

I looked at him, perplexed, and squinted through the smoke. "I love you, though maybe, I am not *in love* with you."

"I feel the same way, darling." He flippantly looked over his shoulder, and opened the back door. "Are you coming?"

I stood frozen, leaning against the railing of the deck. A slight breeze blew my dress against my legs. "Yes. I'm coming."

We entered the kitchen where voices carried from the living room. Irving pulled potatoes with rosemary out of the oven, and I helped him plate the dishes. The smell of the food steaming brought everyone to the dining room without a word. All six sat around the table, wine glasses in hand.

"Irving and I have made a decision," announced Nico, breaking the initial silence of good food. "We are going to be married at Burning Man."

"What?" I laughed nervously.

"Oh yes. But of course, we will never consummate it, being that Irving is so hetero."

Irving laughed with glee as everyone looked at them with confusion.

"You see, this way we'll be able to adopt a daughter from Cuba together," Nico explained.

"We are adopting a daughter from Cuba," added Irving for emphasis.

"What the hell are you talking about?" asked Miriam.

Irving jumped in. "Well, we figure since neither of us will ever be with just one woman, it would be much simpler if we adopted a child together."

"And all the different women in our lives could play different roles."

"They can all baby-sit!"

"Just think. One hundred different mothers."

"She'll be the most messed up child ever," I said, shaking my head.

"No, she'll be well rounded," replied Irving.

"So, you're going to have a woman you're involved with baby-sit while you go out to get laid? Oh that will work!" Miriam waved her hand through the air.

"What makes you think the women would be into that? It would completely disrupt your lifestyle," added George.

"Exactly! We could all unite more fully in order to raise a child."

"And we could share all the women, since we will be married and united in our journey," added Irving.

"Of course, by the time she turns seventeen I don't think I would be able to consider her my child anymore. You know," said Nico

George shook his head. "Disgusting."

Irving and Nico smiled at each other in a way that made it impossible to tell if they were serious. Turning to me, Nico's eyes had the look of a wild animal, with a hint of the lost child looking for its mother. Just then, I wanted to find him. I could not see where he began and where he ended. Every word that came out of his mouth was something unexpected. Kind of like with Irving, but multiplied.

"Well," said Irving, "I just hope I will be a better father than my own. I just made out my will, and I decided to leave my dad a one-dollar bill. It's more than he deserves."

I wondered over being the only person I knew with a father who didn't desert me, or screw me over somehow. I got up to dish out the pie I had brought, and Irving started berating George for lighting up a joint.

"Lauren is sensitive to that stuff. I don't want you doing that in here!"

"It's okay," I called.

"No it isn't. It messes up her head and makes her depressed. Seriously."

I felt embarrassed that I was being protected. But also surprised that Irving was actually standing up for me and showing that he cared. I sat down, and he swooned over my blueberry pie. In a tired, drunken daze he asked me, "So what if in this moment, I came to you and said, 'I am in love with another woman and we're getting married.'"

"I would have to say, 'sayonara,'" I answered, waving my hand goodbye.

"Well then, you don't really love me, do you? It's all based on your own desires. You don't know how to love without claiming something for your own." He looked as though he might begin to cry.

Miriam jumped in, "No, it wouldn't be selfish. She wants to protect your love relationship and doesn't want to cause mistrust in your partner. Lauren's feelings would interfere and cause temptation for you."

Irving looked down at his wine glass, "I am often too intense for people to take."

"So am I," I replied.

There was a look of recognition in his eye. "You know, we could marry under certain circumstances," he said.

I smiled at him and said nothing. But all I could think was, 'Under circumstances I couldn't take.'

After everyone left I lounged on the guest bed stroking Francesco, as Irving scrolled through pictures on the computer. I began to hum "Embraceable You."

Irving was silent. He finally turned to me and said, "This relationship is very sexually frustrating for me."

"Well, I am dealing with that too."

"I am feeling very desirous of you."

We looked at the cat, glanced at each other and then time went into slow motion. He came towards me, holding back from joining me on the bed. We kissed with our fingers pinching the flesh beneath our clothes.

"I should go," I said, getting up.

We stood there in each other's arms. I felt him hard against my thigh. I began to walk away. My mind was headed for the stairs, but my body wanted to go into the bedroom. I followed my head.

As I walked out the front door Irving called, "An excellent performance of chastity!" clapping his hands spastically.

"Brava! Brava!"

Chapter 19

I went to the closet and picked out a black skirt, black shirt and black shoes - my uniform for work. In spirit, I was a highly successful writer. In reality, I worked as a hostess so I could spend my days in coffee shops, reading and writing. I gravitated toward restaurant work because it attracted anarchists, pervs, ne'er do well's, adrenaline junkie's – people I could relate to. But not even hosting was going well.

On the local high school's prom night we were slammed with teenagers in sequins and rentals. As I moved two tables together to accommodate them, I broke a bottle of garlic olive oil. It slid off the corner of the table and crashed onto the fireplace mantel. The stench was like a garlic bomb going off. I haphazardly cleaned it up, too busy to ask for help. The next day the manager slipped on it and fell on her ass.

"Why didn't you get a busser to clean it up?" she asked.

From then on I was relegated to weekends only. The manager was middle-aged, ugly as hell, and miserable. At the end of each night when I asked to clock out, she would often say something demeaning like, "Why don't you just strut back and forth a few more times and give the customers something to look at."

I've never had a decent female manager. My male managers have all been trusting and solid, respectful and able to let me do my thing. The women have all micro-managed, treated me like an idiot or a piece of meat, and couldn't wait for some excuse to take me down a notch; victims creating more victims.

At that particular restaurant, ninety percent of the customers were regulars from the neighborhood. The winery in town had summer concerts, and once in a while a famous band would stop by, or a film director who lived in the neighborhood would turn up.

One regular looked like an over-baked soap opera star. He liked to smoke cigars and swirled his wine like a pro. He went through a phase where he turned up with a different Internet date every Friday night. We never saw him with the same girl twice. One woman especially did not look like she would score a second date. She was all buttons, all the way up to her neck. And yet the buttons appeared they were ready to pop. A real stuffed sausage. They barely talked. But when they left, his car remained, headlights glaring directly into the front window. His windows steamed up, and the vehicle was literally bouncing. We all laughed over it for weeks.

Then there was Tommy, a regular at the bar. He owned several porn sites and wanted me to write erotica for only twenty-five dollars a story. Meanwhile he was making millions and spending six months of the year in the Bahamas. He was in his sixties, thin and attractive with stylish glasses. I loved to hang out with him after work, but as our perverse banter progressed, it became awkward. I realized he had feelings for me, so I began to avoid him.

My favorite server was Otto. He was an older Hungarian man who didn't have much difficulty passing for an Italian. Robust, with many dishes of pasta behind him, he wore glasses with thick black rims and combed his hair back on his head. His wafting cologne competed with the permanent smell of garlic that hung in the air. All the other servers were jealous of him because he got the most customer requests to sit in his section. He enjoyed saying perverse things to the customers, and always got away with it because he had a charming European flair.

To the people that worked there though, Otto's tight space fondles and whispers in the ear got old quick. Not for me, however. I appreciated his depraved sense of humor and lust for life. In quiet moments he cut the act and had more serious conversations with me, about life and love.

"I've been married fifteen years," he'd say, "and I've never cheated on my wife. Not once. Open relationships are bullshit. Bullshit, bullshit, bullshit! One day you wake up and you realize you don't know each other. There's no trust."

I thought so too. Monogamy was important for a serious relationship, but I'd never had one. I didn't see the point if you were just having fun.

"You have a boyfriend?" he asked.

"Eh," I replied, wavering my hand so-so.

"Part-time!" he exclaimed. "When's the last time you've done it?"

"Lets see... June."

"Son of a bitch!" he exclaimed.

"I know. Two months. I think I've lost my pizzazz."

"Nah. Honey, you haven't lost a thing. You've still got it!" he said, pinching my arm and winking.

Otto was the only co-worker that I connected with. Whereas my fellow hostess didn't like the live band we hired because their songs didn't have words. She cringed over fresh flowers because they made her sneeze. She was the sort of person who could eat chicken fingers out of a frozen box everyday of her life and not realize she was missing anything. The other women were much older with marriages and kids in high school. And the kitchen guys were just perverted.

My favorite dish was penne con gorgonzola e prosciutto. But everyday when my shift was over and it was time to order the penne, they gave me a hard time.

"Where is my penne?" I asked.

Fernando pointed to his crotch, "It's right here, but I'm not sure if you want it, cause it's pretty small!"

"You know what penne means in Spanish?" asked Raul.

"I just figured it out," I replied.

"What are you going to do when you get home? Watch porno movies?" asked Raul.

"No. I live with my parents! I got rid of all my porn."

One day Raul came up behind me when I was in the office getting pencils. He grabbed my arm hard and wouldn't let go. Blocking my path, he tried to close the door.

"Let me go, Raul!" I laughed out of nervousness.

"No, no, no, no. I've got you now!" he said into my face.

"No, you don't. Stop it. I mean it," I said, getting serious.

One of the bussers came around the corner, and he dropped my arm. I fled. Before I left that night I told my manager what happened. The next week Raul was gone.

"He was fired," my co-hostess said.

"What happened?" I asked.

"I guess he was using drugs. Dealing them too," she replied.

Whether it was drugs or his attempt to trap me in the office, I felt safe again in the kitchen. Everyone *else* had boundaries. And maybe the owner had a talk with the kitchen guys, because they didn't make as many cracks anymore. After a while, I got sick of penne and got on a calamari kick. I preferred to have Fernando, the sous chef, make it for me. The other guy who made it was new - John, a white guy still in his teens. His calamari wasn't nearly as good. One night, I sat at the bar and the bartender brought over my calamari. It was the best I'd ever had.

"Who made the calamari tonight?" I asked the bartender. "John."

"Are you kidding? It's amazing. This is the best ever."

It might have been the last dish that John ever made. That night he hung himself. His girlfriend had left him and moved out. He was depressed. They say that in suicide cases, on the last day of your life you try to do your best, knowing it will be your last. I avoided the kitchen for weeks after that, and lost my taste for calamari.

Chapter 20

We were feeling lazy. Going kayaking had sounded like an exciting expedition. But once Irving remembered what a struggle it was to dig into the garage, hose off the kayaks, load the equipment, and strap the kayaks to the roof of the car it became a chore. We arrived at Alki Beach and shoved offshore towards Blake Island. I did my best to keep up with Irving, but then his phone rang, piercing the peaceful lull of waves and distant birds.

"You brought your cell phone?"

"Just keep paddling. I'll catch up with you."

"You're kidding me!"

As I paddled at a fast pace, his conversation went on and on. Distracted, I failed to notice a ship approaching, directly in front of my path. The enormity of it unnerved me. I wished that Irving were beside me as I remembered a time when a ship had crossed the path of a speedboat I had been in. The first wave had been taller than the boat. It came crashing down on top of us as five more followed in its path. Everything was soaked.

Luckily, I was so close to the ship that as the waves came

they hadn't crested. Facing them head-on, it was easy to maneuver across. Looking back I watched Irving struggle as the waves rolled and broke into four-foot waves. He had deserved that one. Catching up alongside we soon approached shore.

"Now be careful that you don't tip over when you roll in."

"Sure," I said, annoyed by his condescending tone.

The waves pushed us in and my kayak slid smoothly into the sand, while Irving lost his balance and flipped over. I laughed as he dragged himself out, grabbing his waterproof sack.

"Shit! My cell phone got wet!" he fumed.

"Good! You shouldn't have brought it with you."

"I don't think its working!" he exclaimed. He tried to call his friend, and nothing happened. "Damn it!"

"Forget about your phone, and just enjoy life. You're never in the moment, always anticipating something. Waiting for the next night, the next party, the next call. Just enjoy being with me."

"I enjoy you very much."

"*Be* with me then."

"I am."

"No. No you're not," I said, dragging the kayak across the sand. I collapsed with my legs crossed. "I can't see past the wall with you."

He slapped the bag down, pinched his lips to the side, and stretched out on the hot sand. "Well darling. I *am* enjoying myself."

I laid back next to him, "I don't want to nag you. I just want you to be aware of how you make me feel."

He puckered his lips beckoning me to kiss him and then backed away when I dove in. I was angry, but then he held me and said, "I do care for you."

I kissed his cheek and felt an unbearable sense of desire. Lying back down, he put on his sunglasses, looked in my direction, and smiled.

We pretended to take a nap. I dug my legs into the hot sand, squinting under a thin layer of sweat, trying to focus further on the sound of waves. All I wanted was to take off my clothes and completely bare myself in a wild expression of freedom. The sounds of children playing behind us disrupted my thoughts. The more Irving held back, the more I wanted to possess him. I felt angry for the way he made me feel. Turning on my side I watched Irving breathe. His shades curved upwards giving him a devilish appearance. I imagined that he was thinking of another woman.

"Lauren."

"What."

"I'm tired of reality."

"What do you mean? You lead a perfect reality. Boring job that makes a lot of money, nice house, good food, lovely cats, endless parties, an abundance of women, and practically anything you want."

"Maybe I'm just tired of everything. But you're right. I lead a rich life, full of beautiful women. I love women, Lauren.

"I know Irving. Women make you happy. But too much of a good thing isn't a good thing anymore." I rolled onto my back and Irving squinted at me through the sun.

"It's kind of like looking at magazines," I said. "I don't want to see beautiful women anymore. All these beautiful women appear to have empty heads, playing a submissive or dominant role. It's so fake. I want to see interesting women. Interesting is erotic. I find myself being more drawn to the people behind the scenes, the photographers and artists, the people who have faces that speak."

"We need to head back," Irving said lazily. I could tell he hadn't been listening.

"I wish we could stay on the island till dusk. But I'm hungry."

We sat up in the sand in our shorts and t-shirts watching the waves lick up the shore and fall back down. The sound usually relaxed me, but I felt agitated instead.

"Irving, I'm tired of reality too. I wish I could really be with you."

He looked straight ahead and took my hand. We sat silently looking out across the water to the city on the other side.

"Lets get going." Irving said, as he glanced at me sideways. His eyebrows were pressed together with tension.

We shoved off from shore, racing back to the mainland, invigorated by the air of the sea and boats passing by. Irving looked quite alive, and I felt happy again. He grinned at me.

"Lauren, it was amazing. I was at a party in the forest last weekend. Everyone was dancing around this wild bonfire, all barely clothed and glowing from the heat. It was so sexually exciting, and I strongly felt that we were all unified, all these sweating, writhing bodies dancing. Everyone was so beautiful and sexual, it made me wish I had twenty dicks so that I could have sex with all of them at once."

"What a strange visual image! You would look like a fountain."

A sly look came across his face. "Imagine a woman with twenty vaginas. It would be so hard to choose which one to plunge into."

"Disgusting. Can you imagine? It's like a fantasy right out of Marquis De Sade."

"Ah! My idol."

"I hope not."

"Lauren, you are a pleasure to corrupt."

"You know, I have this theory that women have a higher capacity for sex, and men have a higher capacity for lust," I said.

"I don't know about that."

"I almost think that you enjoy imagining these things more than actually having sex."

Irving shook his head, "That's not true. But I do enjoy anticipation."

We paddled in silence. The sun was setting behind us and the space needle loomed majestically; a remnant of what the future is supposed to look like. The Olympic Mountains stood solemnly to the east.

"I don't want to reach the shore. It means our day will end," I said.

"There will be other days." Irving was silent for a

moment and then asked, "How many guys from your past are still in your life?"

"None."

"Exactly. But I am staying."

When we arrived back at Irving's house, his friend Victor was waiting on the doorstep.

"Where were you man, I've been waiting and waiting."

"My phone broke."

They were going to a party, but I wasn't invited. Victor came in and sat on the couch while I went upstairs with Irving. In the walk-in, his eyes glazed over as he smoked a joint. He was far away again and I was tired of all the feelings he made me feel. He held the joint out to me, suddenly forgetting what he'd said to George the other night, and how it messes up my head and makes me depressed.

"No thanks. How about the furry vest?"

"Not in the mood for fur. I'm feeling polyester," he said, pulling out his favorite shirt with the big orange flowers. He slipped it on with the joint hanging from his mouth. I found him so beautiful with his dark hair and skin set off by his clothes. But a wave of exhaustion followed, knowing he would be with someone else that night.

"Irving, thank you for taking me kayaking. I have to go," I said, as our lips brushed. His eyes were a blurry cloud. I looked away towards the white wall trying my best to feel nothing.

Chapter 21

On my 21st birthday I ordered a chocolate martini at Joe Bar in Portland. My parents had let me drink wine before, but this was my first taste of liquor. I took one sip and immediately began to feel a gentle tingling in my vagina. It was extraordinary. Here we were in this very chic bar on a black leather banquette with stunning art and stunning people all around us and I wanted more of it, all of it. I felt alive.

A week later we were at Panorama, a huge gay club with three dance floors. One room had a fog machine with giant blocks that created a tower. Men with their shirts off danced on the blocks, sweaty and beautiful, flowing in one rhythm that seemed endless, circling back on itself. Depeche Mode boomed through the speakers. *"Words are very unnecessary. They can only do harm."*

I danced up behind a perfect specimen and moved my body against his back. For the entirety of the song he didn't turn around, just held onto me from behind. I liked the way he smelled. He turned and we were moving as one. There was a solid feeling in him, from his arms, to his back, even to his penis. I craved it. My life had been all female - all flesh, reproach, judgment, feelings, drama, cycles, insecurity, over-analyzation. Here was something that felt like a rock. I hung on for dear life. I didn't care if beneath the muscles he had no substance, at least not until the music ended.

Predictably, at closing time they played, "Last Dance." He kissed me. It was my first kiss. I wasn't sure what to do with my tongue, so I just circled it around his slowly. At first it seemed tricky, but then I let the feeling take over.

When the song ended we sat on a banquette waiting for our friends. It turned out he was still married but was getting a divorce. He couldn't have been much older than I was. He worked at Les Schwab, lifting tires all day.

The lights came up, and along with it, my fantasy of the mysterious stranger. I knew I would never talk to him again. But I liked the adrenaline rush of not knowing whom I was kissing. I loved the feeling of being wanted for no other reason than how I looked, and how I danced. It felt primal and basic and visceral. I had never met someone who could understand my thoughts, and probably never would.

Chapter 22

I was having dinner with Irving on Lake Union. The moon was full; its reflection kissed the tips of waves that rocked sailboats. The glittering skyline was a distant celebration that we were not invited too. I nibbled on shrimp covered in spicy fruit salsa. Candlelight flickered.

Irving recounted his latest conquest. "I invited her to Burning Man, and at first I thought I was crazy for doing it. I mean, who does that when you can have anyone you want? But I didn't want anyone else. The whole thing culminated in this one grand public fuck on the very last night. The man was burning, and we did it right in the sand, as people passed us by. Nico was off somewhere with a trail of followers. And all I could focus on were Leila's perfect breasts bouncing up and down. She modeled for Playboy once."

"Hasn't everyone?" I said sarcastically.

"So I really thought that I could be monogamous with Leila," Irving continued.

I erupted into nervous laughter, insulted that he had never felt this way about me.

"Go ahead. Laugh. She did too. She laughed in my face."

"Really," I replied, "Maybe I like her more than I first thought."

"She said, 'No way.' I haven't seen her since. What came over me?"

"I don't know, but the girls you date seem to be getting younger and younger."

"No. Younger and dumber," he replied.

"It sounds like she's intelligent to me."

Irving tensed up. "Women my age only want security. By the time they hit thirty they disconnect from the substance of life and go into survival mode. Men are much more romantic than that."

"Maybe they are connecting, but can't be with someone who is so disconnected from himself."

Irving bit a shrimp off from its tail and chewed delicately, looking at me with disapproval.

"They lack adventure," he stated.

"That's quite a generalization. I think they just know what they want and are no longer willing to dick away their time with someone like you. I mean, where can it lead?" Anger leapt with insensitivity off my tongue. Irving looked out over the water and up to the sky.

"There's a full moon tonight."

"It's so romantic!" I pretended to swoon, tossing my head with the back of my hand pressed to my forehead.

"It makes me feel the warm fuzzies for you all over again. Anyway, my ex-wife is getting remarried."

"Oh!"

"She called and told me two weeks ago."

"So that's why you thought you could be with Leila. You're mourning the finality of your separation."

"I guess so. I can't believe she's marrying him. He's a real drag. I asked her if she loves him and she goes, 'Well... you know. It's different.'"

"What a strange answer."

"She feels safe. She's less adventurous now. And so it goes."

"She's just one person. And after you, I could see why she

would want a little more safety now."

"Anyway, I'm going to the wedding. Not looking forward to it though. I have nothing in common with the guy. I met him once a year ago."

"Well then. What are you competing against? She doesn't even sound happy."

"I feel what you said. A sort of finality."

Later on at the house we sat down on the couch with some tea. I enjoyed this new openness that Irving was sharing with me. I rested my head on his knee and stared at the wooden couples copulating in the distance.

"I can breathe again when I'm here with you," I sighed. The words sounded scripted and I couldn't believe I said them out loud. Embarrassment flushed my cheeks. I had the intense desire to wrap myself around Irving though I was also afraid to touch him.

The pressure was overwhelming. I could feel his desire for me like an electrical surge. I stood up and walked to the door. Irving followed, took my hand and drew me into him. I stumbled over his feet, and we laughed. But then in silence, the proximity overtook us. He looked into my eyes and saw that it was painful for me to be so near him. He breathed in deeply and ran his fingers through my hair. He kissed my nose, forehead and each cheek. We stood there, forgetting the circumstance, and then we kissed.

A charge of breath rushed up and caught in my throat. I closed my eyes and relaxed the muscles in my face. Then I exhaled, breathed him in, and remembered. The pain dove down and hit my gut. Tears welled, sobs constricted through my neck. I choked into his shirt and he held me tightly to keep me from shaking.

"I don't know where that came from."

He led me back to the couch. "It's okay."

We stared at the coffee table topped with Irving's artfully arranged books. We held hands with our legs crossed like two bookends mirroring each other.

"Is there anything that you want to talk about?" he asked.

I said nothing.

"I'm so intensely physically and intellectually attracted to you. But I'm just not good for you right now."

"I'm sorry I cried."

"No, thank you for crying. It..."

"It woke you up."

"It was good. I just feel too vulnerable tonight." Irving turned, "You know, I'm going to Europe for a month. It will be good for us to be apart. We shouldn't talk for a while."

"Yes... I don't remember who I was before you. Who am I now?"

"You are wonderful any way you are. You're beautiful and intelligent. You stimulate my intellect, and that is really more rare than anything."

I started to think that Leila had probably never stimulated his intellect, but Leila was the one he wanted. I felt cheated, yet could not voice any of this since our clandestine moments were coming to an end. The minutes slipped by, falling through the cracks. As I walked through the front door we took each other's hands with furtive glances. I turned away and let go before desire could take control. I walked up the sidewalk and heard Irving shut the door behind me. Unlocking the car I fell into the driver's seat. I turned the key in the ignition and rolled off the clutch, feeling too dead and more alive than I knew how to be.

Chapter 23

*"Jealousy leaves no time to be bored;
does it even leave time to grow old?"*

Colette

I arrived late Sunday afternoon to Irving's birthday party where various eccentric females milled about stirring mojitos. Exhausted and hung over, Irving stood against the counter wearing rubber sandals, a red sarong, and a black tank. It was the exact same outfit that I remembered Nico wearing just a month ago and it seemed pathetic of Irving to copy Nico's style. At the same time, however, his weakness was endearing. I bravely entered a circle of people in the kitchen.

"I work in a chiropractor's office. But I'm going back to school for fashion design," said a mousy woman.

"I'm returning for architecture, myself," replied the guy next to her.

"I thought about architecture. But fashion is more my thing," she responded.

I attempted to jump in, "I was a fashion major as well!"

The fashion girl glared at me for a brief second and then

looked down at her mojito. Turning back to the others she continued, "Yes, I have a lot of work to do before school."

I didn't want to be there. Judging by the extreme ratio, about thirty women to five men, it was obvious that Irving's motive was to watch women compete for him. My mind traveled from the conversation and faded into the background where I spotted the small present I brought for Irving. Picking it up I walked over to him in the dining room.

"Is this for me?"

"Well, it's your birthday!"

"This is beautiful. Just look at the symbolism," he fingered the collaged envelope, the straw string, reading the note inside.

"Kiss me," he threw his arms around me, and our lips met across a chair between us. I lost my fear of jealousy as I drank in the sensory experience of his body.

"And what is this? A book. *The Pure and the Impure* by Colette. I haven't read this one yet."

"It's my favorite novel."

"I remember," he nodded.

"You should take it to bed with you, instead of all those girls."

"My grandmother used to say that," he laughed. He looked at me through a long awkward pause. Sifting emotions, searching.

Shrill voices burst through the door and Irving turned away. I stood and watched the parade of kisses and ecstatic glances - each girl trying to be louder and more entertaining than the next. I went to the kitchen and gathered food on a plastic plate, and sat in the corner of the living room, surveying all the women Irving chose to sleep with. I felt nauseous. Next to me a man listened quietly to the girl across from us. She looked lost on the sofa with the frailty of an invalid.

"I'm realizing how much my world can expand. People limit themselves too much. If only they opened their minds, they could understand so much more."

"I know what you mean. People are generally afraid of all

102

that."

"I just love these photography books," the girl said, "I'm doing landscapes with a slight watercolor look."

I turned to her, "I did some photos using my body as a landscape. They turned out really well. One of them looked like the Sahara dessert; all rolling hills, though it was really just my thighs, hips and knees."

"I used to do some erotic art. My roommate and I ended up being the photographers and the subjects. Now she's moved out, but I'd like to do more with it," she said, looking distant. "Irving has such good taste in photography. He's really very cultured."

"So how do you know Irving?" I asked.

"I met him last night actually," she looked down, "With that other girl, what's her name again?" She pointed across the room at a girl with a bleach blonde pixie cut.

"I haven't met her," I said.

"I haven't been home yet."

The man next to me raised his eyebrows and smiled at me in recognition - we were both contemplating the odd threesome that must have occurred.

"I'm bad with names," the girl said.

"Me too," I added.

The mojito was weighing me down. My head felt heavy, and my stomach churned. "I think I need some fresh air," I said, leaving them behind. I was trying not to feel angry over a houseful of lovers for the one man I still loved. Irving was lounging on the back lawn, surrounded by six fawning women. I glided between the adoring glances, and sat by his side without hesitation. He was the only one oblivious to my presence, and waves of tension rose. Vocal chords struck with trepidation. No one knew anyone besides Irving, and how many others *were* there? Some of the women digressed to the kitchen and Irving disappeared with them. The man from the living room sat beside me. His name was Peter and he wore a hound's-tooth hat and horn-rimmed glasses. He had a cozy look about him that made me feel safe for the first time all day.

"I love your hat, by the way."

"Thanks. So how do *you* know Irving?"

"Can I tell you the truth? I've never told one of his friends the truth before. I'm supposed to tell you this believable lie that we met salsa dancing."

"I'll take the truth. Promise I won't tell."

"I just feel too real with you to lie. We met through an internet dating service last February."

"Really!"

"We dated for a while, and then moved on for obvious reasons."

"Obvious reasons?"

"Wouldn't anyone grow sick of competing with this menagerie?" I extended my arm to present the panoramic view of the women all around us.

Peter stared at me blankly, as though he didn't understand. "So I take it this is your first polyamorous relationship?"

"Polyamorous?" I asked.

"Open to other people?" he prodded.

"I guess so, at least he was. I wasn't really interested in other people, unfortunately."

Irving appeared once again, toting a female entourage and two distant cousins. One was rather collegiate and athletic, while the father had gray hair, glasses, and a prominent nose. Irving resumed his place on my right, and I forgot about Peter sitting to the left.

"So Irving, how is your mother doing? How old is she now?" asked the older cousin with his legs and arms all crossed.

"She is sixty-five now. Why don't you try a drink?

"Oh, I don't touch the stuff."

"One sip won't hurt you. It just tastes of lime."

The older cousin took a brief sip and handed the red plastic cup back to Irving. "Not bad."

A short blonde woman pranced into the gathering, lying back with her head resting on Irving's lap. She squinted up at me with the eyes of a territorial cat.

"You know, Irving never had a Bar mitzvah," said the older cousin.

"Really! Well that explains so much then," I burst out. "Why would Irving ever want to celebrate the responsibility that comes with being a man?"

A few people laughed, then were cut off by a shriek from the top of the stairs, "Irving!"

All heads turned to the deck where a woman pranced conspicuously down the stairs and across the lawn. She bobbed back and forth.

"Edible body paint! I've been making guacamole!" She pushily motioned for Irving to lick the green gunk off her fingers, and though a bit agitated by the volume of her voice, he obliged. She was dressed in beach clothes, tan with long blonde hair, and a piercing in her bottom lip that accentuated prominent buckteeth. Her voice was low and gravelly.

"I'll be back with more!" In a few moments she reappeared in different clothes, jeans and a top. Then she made another disappearance, and returned with yet another ensemble. This time she wore a tightly tailored designer top, buttoned only at the center of her black bra, with black slacks and black designer stilettos. She called them her sex shoes, her ultimate fetish, the pair made for creating an entire lifestyle around. It seemed that in her numerous changes of clothing she was trying to embody Irving's desire for novelty and lots of women. She stood in front of the cousins, in front of Irving, me, and Peter, to describe her trip to Italy, accentuating the persistence of constant sexual pursuit.

"And I went to the beach and they go," putting her hands in the air in great big gestures, 'You are soooooo beeeeuuuuutyful! You are sooo beeuutyful!'" She stopped for a short breath, "And amazing how their soccer ball just happened to land next to me at the beach. And they go, 'Come play ball with us.' And I'm like, 'Sorry boys, but I'm not touching *any* of *your* balls!'"

The older cousin shifted uncomfortably in his seat. As she paced, the sky-high heels aerated the lawn until finally she sat down to share her expertise on the art of vomiting.

"You go past the sink, past the bidet. Baby, it's the bathtub every time. I didn't puke from the age of sixteen to twenty-one. Oh shit, last time on the airplane I was downing Bailey's and then my friends took me out and I was a mess. The bathtub is perfect. You throw-up, you wash it down, put your head under the faucet and peel off the clothes. They're all like knocking on the door and I'm all, 'Just need a little privacy here!'"

"Wow. I haven't thrown up in eight years," I said, remembering my last bout with stomach flu.

"Knock on wood, once you say it, it's gonna happen."

"Ugh." breathed Peter. By this point Irving had quietly disappeared.

"So where are you from?" Peter asked her.

"I grew up in New York City. My brother passed away in the World Trade Center."

"Sorry to hear that."

"Yeah, nobody's moving to Manhattan right now." She went silent for a moment. Then she drifted off again and reappeared in another pair of jeans.

My mouth dropped open. "Another outfit? I can't believe it!"

"We all have our vices," Peter replied.

Just then Nico magically appeared through the back door and bounded down, leaping across the grass to kiss me. Laughter spilled from my lips.

"Oh, Lauren! I want to see you soon! I want to make love to you too! But we can just have fun!"

"You're way too dangerous," I giggled.

He shared his excitement over the Tiramisu he had made covered in hydrangea buds and red currants with a layer of marzipan that read, "Buon Compleanno Irving." More people came and went and the blonde soon left in her fifth outfit. I overheard Nico telling the girl across from me about the day of Summer Solstice when he and Irving had sex with a woman named Lexi.

"So Irving was doing her, and I was licking her and you should have seen him go flying backwards when I accidentally licked his penis!"

I turned in the direction of a pointed finger and saw Lexi, a short and abundant woman with a flat nose, dressed in an oversized nurse's uniform with heavy looking black boots. I was certain that Nico told the story within earshot to make sure that I heard it. Repulsion washed over me and nausea sent me to the front door. I slipped out and stood on the steps, surrounded by Irving's flowers, breathing in the cool air away from the risk of the crowd. There was nothing really here, to feel jealous of. I was envious of no one. How can you be jealous if you're not envious? All of these women seemed pathetic and desperate. And for what? I wasn't sure exactly, anymore.

From inside I heard the announcement, "It's time to spank the Birthday boy!"

My eyebrows shot up and I spun around, flying over the front steps. Blocking my path was a mop topped busty broad with fake money hanging out of a bikini under a little jacket. With a scrunched up face, she grimaced at me as I dashed around her through the living room. All eyes turned to Irving and up went the red sarong, down went the boxer briefs. The spanking woman draped him over her lap. I overheard that she was a professional dominatrix. Her maternal bosoms fell across his back, pointing towards the cleavage of his ass.

I stepped up to bat, ready to slam my hand down hard. But it only came down with a friendly slap. A succession of partygoers followed, whacking kitchen utensils down upon burning red skin as the spanking woman repeated, "It's only pink, he needs more!"

Finally, he'd had enough. Kneeling off her lap, he reassembled the sarong and devilishly decided to smack a kiss onto each and every guest, beginning with Peter, followed by me, and ending with all the others. Kissing a man with a goatee, a blonde chirped, "You've expanded my world again! I never knew it would be so sexy to see two men with goatees kiss!"

Nico finally had all the attention, and led the crowd in singing, "Buon Compleanno Irving." The cake was massacred and guests fed chunks of espresso-soaked ladyfingers, mascarpone, and currants to Irving with their fingers. They licked the cake off his face, and kissed him some more.

Everyone quickly dispersed back into their circles, and salsa music began. Irving turned to me, "I want to dance with you." He took my hand and led me to the center of the room. His perspiration seeped into my skin as our bodies locked and swayed. He spun me across the floor with ease. I could trust his hands to catch me. It was the one time that he was the dancing partner I'd always wanted him to be. I was happy, and desperate to leave before the bubble burst.

"I have to leave now, but I'll be right back." I ran to say goodbye to Nico.

"Call me, call me!" Nico exclaimed. He kissed me, kissed me again, and then kissed me passionately. I opened my eyes in shock, and for a glimpse of a second saw a row of women staring.

I pulled away, "I must go!"

I wandered back to Irving, who held me close.

"You know, you were the most elegant woman here tonight," he whispered into my ear.

"I've heard that before," I smiled. The tips of our fingers brushed as we let go, and I drifted away from him, looking back as I stepped into the night. The music sounded far away, and I breathed in, alone where no one could hurt me. Irving would be leaving for his trip in just a few days.

Chapter 24

Two weeks after my first kiss, I had to go back to
Panorama. When my friends and I first arrived, an annoying
guy wouldn't stop following me with his spluttering Corona.
From room to room, he reappeared. I climbed up onto the
blocks trying to disappear between the beautiful bodies of gay
men. But the guy followed, grasping at me clumsily from
behind.

Below me I saw a beaming boy who danced as though he
didn't care what anyone thought of him. He moved his arms
expansively and shook his body – alone, happy and golden.
Here was my ticket to dissuade the grasper. I jumped down to
the floor, and came fe to face with my freedom.

We flailed together for a long time, just smiling. I
wondered if he was gay. But then we were grasping,
clutching, swallowing each other. His neck smelled like
violets, his sweat so fresh and salty I drank it in. His hands
curved into me beneath my pants and I rolled into him. I
wondered where my friends were. I hoped that none of them
could see, but I also didn't really care.

At the end of the night, I found out his name was Erik.

He told me that he was a trombonist in a famous band. They were number two on the pop charts in Paris for a French chanson. I didn't really believe him. On the street he gave me a chaste kiss on the cheek, as though nothing else had happened. Inside the club we had left our lives behind. Outside, we were ourselves – shy, insecure, and nervous.

In the next two weeks we talked on the phone for hours. He confessed that he loved the ballet, gardening and flower arranging. His soccer buddies teased him for it. He was busy jet setting with the band and took a short trip to Paris for publicity. A French journalist flirted with him and he regaled me with all of his witty responses.

"I should learn French, it's so sexy," he said. I felt jealous.

I left for a five-week student trip through Europe thinking I would lose him. Five weeks seemed like forever. I wrote him postcards, caught up in my own romantic fantasy of a person I had only met once. I bought his band's CD and everywhere we went I heard their single on the radio. At the Virgin Records in Paris I was shocked to find that there must have been a hundred copies of their CD and a huge cardboard display. I felt a sense of pride that my life had intertwined with this music that was so popular in Paris. To everyone else, they were just songs, but to me, they were Erik.

I replayed the night we met over and over in my head through train rides, uncomfortable beds with flat pillows, ruins and ancient cathedrals. I remembered how even the day after I met him, while taking a nap, the muscles in my lips were still in motion from our kiss. Though we had said goodbye twelve hours prior, it felt as though he was still there.

When I returned home from the trip, exhausted and very ill, I found a card from him with a photo of a tulip on the front. He asked me to come visit him and spend the night before a long tour that would begin in Tunisia, go through Europe, and end in Lebanon. He mentioned he would have the whole house to himself. On the back of the card he wrote the words of an Argentine tango that took me weeks to translate.

> *"Tonight, Martingale*
> *with the little that we have*
> *I am going to embrace you*
> *yes I am*
> *if it is heads or tails*
> *I am going to embrace you."*

My parents were disappointed in me. They wanted me to stay somewhere else. I had plenty of friends in Portland, why did I have to stay with him? On one hand, I was scared, on the other I no longer wanted to be frightened of life. Maybe I wasn't who I had thought I had been.

I had been the epitome of abstinence, literally abstaining from life. I had laughed at friends in codependent relationships. They found my independent strength intimidating.

When the weekend came, Erik put my friend and I on the guest list for their show in Portland at the Crystal Ballroom. The drinks began to flow, the floor bounced, and finally the band took the stage. Erik looked beautiful in his vintage suit. I watched every little move he made. I counted the amount of times he admired the girls onstage behind him. I noted his nervousness. He seemed stiff. I wondered if it was because I was there.

The set went by fast. As they bowed and played their encores my friend pushed me up front where the band members took their exit. Erik strode off the stage with his glowing trombone. I waved spastically. He dodged over and kissed me, then disappeared through the door. I forgot to breathe.

When I arrived at Erik's house the next day he looked fresh and magnificent. He gave me a friendly hug. I was confused. Were we just friends now? I had been pining for him for months.

We went to pick out a new pair of frames for his glasses and ran into the lead singer of the band, whose boyfriend ran the shop. Then we drove out of the city to hike to some hot springs. I had my swimsuit on beneath my clothes.

When we arrived we heard strange sounds coming from behind the hut. It sounded like a dog, or a child, or maybe even a woman. There was a large group in the first tub, so we walked into the hut. Two older hippies sat naked in the tubs staring up at us with somber eyes. Their penis's floated in the water. We realized then, that we were hearing the sound of people having sex.

"I think I've lost my appetite for the hot springs," said Erik, as we walked over to a picnic table. We ate our ham sandwiches listening to the never-ending orgasm. I began to laugh hysterically. My nervousness flooded out in laughter.

"I can't eat anymore," he said.

We began to walk back. He told me how he and his friend used to play their trombones on the cliffs nearby. I remembered why I liked him, and in the next instant, thought I hated him for being so cold. He was right there, but so far away and locked in his own independence. I was finally with him, lying in wait to feel his arms wrap around my body. I decided there must be something wrong with me. Maybe he didn't find me attractive in daylight. Maybe I was ugly. Or maybe I had revealed too much.

"What is the word love?" he asked suddenly. "In other languages they have twenty words for love. Here we say, I love my dog, I love my sister, I love my mom, I love *you* Lauren. And they all mean different things."

I listened silently, trying to decipher his sudden preoccupation with love. Why would he insert my name into his treatise? Was he teasing me?

Back at the house he showed me photos. I assumed at this point that he would ask me to sleep on the couch. He had yet to touch me. I felt that he was disappointed. I was not who he had thought I was, but neither was he. Our words began to make no sense at all. He started rambling something about the Vietnam War and I couldn't figure out how he got there. His bedroom was all white with Birch logs for bedposts and stacks of music piled on the desk and bookshelves. He sat quietly looking at me with his knees pressed up against his chest.

"I'd like to kiss and cuddle but I don't want anything in the way of a relationship right now," he said.

"I'm okay with that," I instantly replied.

His eyebrows shot up.

"I just have to go to the bathroom," I said, dodging the bedroom. My hands shook as I washed them with ocean fresh hand soap. I came back and sat on the bed.

We pounced. We were in a sprint to the finish line. And then he got up, "Wait, I'm going to turn off the lights. I don't really want to have sex, and we'll talk through this and if anything makes you feel uncomfortable, just let me know and we'll stop."

"Okay."

In my head, nothing could stop me from having sex. I had my bathing suit on under my clothes which made the removal of clothing seem okay. He asked piece by piece if we could take the next item off. And all I remember is his ravenous hunger and how I wanted all of it. We writhed into each other, and he whispered, "Just enjoy the feel of skin against skin."

Somehow we went to sleep without penetration. We slept naked, and I awoke on perfectly fluffy pillows with white curtains billowing over my head. Everything around me was white and pure. Erik's head looked stunning on the pillow next to mine. I watched him sleep for a long time. And then he woke up. We grasped onto each other again without saying a word. I was on top of him, circling my hips, and then I came and came and came. Erik seemed amazed and almost taken aback. I felt vulnerable over my loss of control.

He laid on his side talking to me and I kept trying not to look at his penis, but there it was. I liked it. I loved his body - solid angles and clean lines. As far as my body went, he complained that my hipbones were too sharp.

I asked Erik about all the sheets of music lying around. He said he wished he could get paid to play classical music, and that in truth, he didn't like the popular music of the band he played in. Before, he had played for the Portland Opera.

He talked about going into science, eventually, and scrapping his career as a professional musician. I was surprised by how ungrateful Erik was. Other musicians *dreamed* of having his success. He made success sound depressing.

He said he had to go to rehearsals, and it became clear I wouldn't be spending any more time with him that weekend. I walked him to the bus stop. There was no trombone in his hand, and I wondered if he kept it at the rehearsal space. I became aware that I was not really part of his life and probably never would be.

Next to his confidence, I felt ugly and uncertain, unable to communicate anything of importance. Paralyzed. The bus pulled up. He kissed me, smiled with careless freedom, and disappeared down the aisle.

As I walked back to the house the sun began to beat a hole through my skull. My body had just gained two hundred pounds of emotion. My chest felt heavy, it was hard to breathe. Everything I'd just done had destroyed my ideals. It began to dawn on me who I really was. I was not the dutiful daughter, the good Christian. I was not obedient and never had been. I was a person who questioned what I'd been told, and wanted to discover the world through my own experience. The sterile person with a life based on appearances didn't exist.

I entered Erik's house and all I could do was sit on the couch and stare off into the distance for a half hour. I faced the self that I really was. It was blatant. Something in me was dying, and it was excruciatingly painful, as though my guts were being shredded and replaced with something else.

I felt a flutter at the thought of his touch. I could still feel him - his hunger, his arms encircling me, the rolling of his hips. I wanted to see him again, and stretch our unreality for as long as it could last.

When I arrived home the next day I couldn't help smiling. It disturbed my mother immensely.

"Well, did you sleep with him?"

I smiled.

My mom turned to my dad who was zoned out into the

television. "Say something to her!" she called to him.

He looked up, "She's twenty-one, it's her life now," he reprimanded angrily.

My mother looked defeated. I was surprised by his response. I disappeared into the basement, my sanctuary from having to be someone I wasn't.

Chapter 25

I went to a nightclub called Club Medusa with my new hair stylist, Tony. I originally met him through the same dating service where I met Irving. Tony was too conventional for my taste, and though handsome, I never cared for classic good looks. We didn't have a whole lot to talk about, apart from our various dating adventures. He ended up just cutting my hair and we hung out every now and then. Even so, when I was still dating Irving, he had felt threatened by Tony.

As we walked in, there was Irving having drinks at the bar. I couldn't believe it. Apparently, he hadn't left for Europe yet.

He walked over to us. "Fancy meeting you here, darling."

"Strange you would be here. Tony and I were looking for a guy with an Irving-vibe for me, and then the real thing shows up!"

"Good luck with that. You can't beat the original." He looked down at his cell phone, pretending to be distracted, and walked off awkwardly. At the bar he acted as though he knew everyone.

A few drinks later, we were nearing the end of the night.

I was sucking on a lollipop that I nabbed from the bathroom attendant's basket. A handsome Italian guy came up to me. "I want to dance with you," he said, sloshing his drink on my shirt.

"Too bad. I'm looking for my friend," I replied.

He took me in his arms and held me tightly.

"You're Italian aren't you?" I asked.

"But of course!" he exclaimed, pulling back.

"Italian men are such playboys! I'm so done with all of you!" I proclaimed, holding my hand up to him.

"But of course! Come with me, you won't regret it." He kissed me.

"I want you to let go," I said, firmly.

"But I can't let go."

"Why not?" I asked.

"Because I have a million feelings," he replied.

I stuck the lollipop in my mouth and glared at him.

"Don't you want to be sucking on something better than that lollipop?"

Just then Tony appeared and pulled me away. "Leave it to you to pick up the one Italian guy here.

We left the club and got in Tony's car. "Kiss me," he said. So I did. But there was no feeling between us.

The next weekend I met *more* Italians. It was like they were all magnetized to me. Angelo had an instant thing for me, but he was full of ridiculous lines and it was impossible to really connect. At the end of the first night with him I used my cliché line on him, "Are you a playboy?"

"Are you a playgirl?" he shot back.

"You tell me," I answered.

"You are not a playgirl. I see it in your eyes. They do not lie to me. You are good, not bad. I know you from your eyes."

I left and he called a half an hour later, then the next day. We had coffee the day after that. After about an hour of empty chitchat, I walked him back to his car. He had actually come out to the suburbs to see me.

"You are weird, Lauren."

"That's kind of an insult."

"If you were not weird, I would not like you. Tell me I am weird too, because if I am normal I have no chance."

"Okay Angelo, you are weird." It wasn't a lie.

"Bravo!" He kissed me. "You are my mystery. Do you know why?"

"Why?"

"Love is a mystery," he began to sing, having his own personal Madonna dance party in the Starbucks parking lot.

I was happy to never hear from him again.

Chapter 26

I stood in the hallway and looked into the study where my mom was playing solitaire on the computer. "If you could, would you ever want to meet Erik?" I asked.

"No. I never want to meet him."

I began to cry. I had let her down and my life was no longer going to fit into their ideals of purity, marriage and family. But I felt more pure than I'd ever been before. I stripped it all away in one small act. Now I was a purist – no walls, no repressions, no hiding.

I looked up, and said, "I wouldn't trust you around him anyway."

"You're right not to trust me. I'd embarrass you by asking him why did he have to mess with my daughter!"

I continued to cry and turned around, tucking myself in towards the wall. Then I began to bang my head against it. It felt good. As though banging my head could release the pressure inside. I was done trying to please everyone else. It was time to live my own life.

"Stop that! You'll give yourself a brain tumor!" my mother exclaimed.

"How can banging my head give me a tumor?" I asked.

"I know someone who had that happen to them," she said, with shaky authority.

"So now on top of my emotional problems, I'm going to need brain surgery. What a chore!" I yelled, banging my forehead some more. The consistent shocks against my skull felt so good. Maybe I could bang away the tug of war.

"Stop it Lauren! Stop hitting your head! You're just like your grandmother; so unstable. We really should get you checked for some kind of chemical imbalance. These mood swings of yours are driving me crazy."

Chapter 27

Somehow I wasn't surprised when Nico called and invited me over for dinner. When I arrived it was the same familiar feeling of being out of place. Not certain how to fit in and afraid to expose all that I felt inside.

There were several people over that night. Nico was busy making risotto cakes and shrimp with arugula. He was too preoccupied to introduce me to anyone, so I just sat at the kitchen table and smiled. A pregnant woman was discussing her plans for diaper-less child rearing.

"This is what people have done for centuries."

"Yeah, in jungles and tribes. But what are you going to say when you're in the supermarket, and the kid takes a piss, or even worse!" exclaimed Nico.

"It's about becoming fully in tune with your child and memorizing their schedule and bowel movements."

"That's crazy. I can't even keep track of my own," said the woman to my left.

"Good point," I added.

"Lauren. I don't like your hair curly. You should wear it straight," said Nico, pointing his finger in the air then rubbing his scruffy chin.

"I like it this way," I responded with edge. "This is the way it naturally is."

He turned back to the stove, "Anyway, it's good to be green. My ex-lover uses sea sponges instead of tampons. You know what else she would do? Amazing belly dancer - while lying down she could flip a coin with her belly. Every woman should learn how to do that."

"Maybe every man should too," said the pregnant woman, with disdain.

"If every woman could do that, the belly dancer wouldn't be unique," I replied.

"She's beautiful. But her boyfriend's a fruitcake," said Nico.

"Beautiful women always have fruitcake boyfriends. The ones that look over their shoulder instead of at what's right in front of them," I mused.

"Lauren. Get over it," he snapped.

"I wasn't putting myself in that category."

"But you *are* in that category, so deal with it."

I looked away then glanced back at Nico, as though we were the only two people in the room. I missed Irving, but it felt good to be without him. As though I was back in my own skin, built for being alone and independent. I wasn't sure why loving someone had to make me feel so weak. And after Irving, I knew that I would never try to claim someone again.

Colin, Nico's English housemate looked down at me and smiled. His good looks were disconcerting – chiseled white planes of skin set off by piercing dark blue eyes and black hair. Nico slid his hand across my shoulder, as though to apologize. I was surrounded on all sides by temptation. I didn't want to give in, but I sensed my journey was just beginning.

There is a part of me that has always been a voyeur of my own life. I remain independent, though I masquerade through people, places and cultures – immersing myself in things I don't understand, just to figure out how it all works, how it all feels, how it all ends.

"Have you met my friend Kara?" Nico asked, pointing to the woman sitting next to me at the table.

"No, I haven't. I'm Lauren, nice to meet you," I said, shaking her hand.

"I'm only in town for the weekend," added Kara.

"She's a showgirl in Vegas!" exclaimed Nico.

"A showgirl. Really." I did my best to sound impressed, though I couldn't fathom Kara being on the stage. She looked more like an aging housewife, lost in baggy sweats with deep lines creasing her face. I sensed there was more to her story.

"I do miss Seattle," said Kara.

Soon friends were leaving and I was the only guest left. I sat in the living room looking at erotic photography books. Nico and Colin stood in the doorway with their arms around each other.

"We both want you," stated Nico. My eyebrows jumped up. They stood smiling like two brothers.

"You do?"

"Spend the night with us," said Colin.

"I don't think I could." I was too shocked to take them up on it. Colin just stood there with his head cocked, smiling with his slightly crooked teeth that made him even more disarmingly attractive. Nico was wild eyed, reeking of anarchism and pheromones.

"I just can't. I should go."

"At least let's kiss."

I walked over to them and we all embraced, smiling at each other timidly. Nico kissed me slowly, then Colin, lingering and smooth as butter. Nico and Colin kissed, and back and forth.

"I wish I could stay."

"So do we," they said in unison.

"Well, I have to go. You know, I'm just not sure."

In my car I wondered why I left, smiling to myself all the way home. It felt so good to be desired.

· · ·

"Lauren, I want you to write the story of my life. It has to be told by someone who can write. You see this lizard tattooed on the back of my ear?" asked Nico. We were sitting in his bedroom a week later, drinking red wine. "The lizards were why I ran away from my father. It's how I ended up on the street. I loved lizards. I made a lasso out of a long piece of grass to catch them with. When I caught them I put them in a well filled with dirt and put a board over the top.

"In the afternoon it was too hot to do anything, so everyone slept. I'd slip out to visit my lizards. Lying in the bottom of the well I let them run all across me. It felt so good; I took all my clothes off. One of them bit me right in the ass and I came all over. It was the first time I ever came and I thought there was something wrong with me. I lost my virginity to the lizards."

"Whoa," I said, as though to stop the story right there. But I wanted to hear more.

"My dad caught me out there one day. He was so angry he poured water into the well and drowned all the lizards. Then he beat me. I ran away that night. I didn't know where I was going or what I would do. I just ran and ran until I collapsed and fell asleep in a field.

"I ended up in Rome and I drew pictures of the sights on the streets to make money from tourists. But the nuns always tried to stop me from doing it. So instead I learned how to give blowjobs. I was begging on a corner and a guy said he would give me money if I would do something for him. He took me down an alley and pulled out his dick. Months later, there was another man that beat me. I hated him. So a long time went by earning money like this, and then I was accused of a crime I didn't commit."

"What was the crime?"

Nico acted as though he hadn't heard me, "They said I could either go to jail or join the French Foreign Legion. So I chose the Legion. They turned me into a fighting machine, and I was a paratrooper. You know how I got out alive from the Legion? I had no fear. I had nothing to lose. Nothing. The minute you are afraid – that's when the bullet hits you. It's all a fucking mind game. I always saw it in their eyes just before they were hit. I learned to not get close to anyone."

"That is crazy."

"When I came here I didn't know how to function in the world. I ordered a root beer at Dick's because I thought it was beer. I was furious that they wouldn't give me a beer, so I reached through the window, grabbed the guy by the collar and pulled him through onto the ground. I was fucked in the head.

"My wife brought me. I deserted to be with her. She was the first woman I had ever been with, and she was American. I didn't tell her a thing about my life. It all added up to lies. That's why I tell everyone everything now."

"That must have been hard, to live with her, without her knowing."

"You know, Lauren. I have been with over a hundred women. I run into them wherever I go. Seattle is a very small world."

"I can imagine," I said, not quite believing him.

"But I never once cheated on my wife. After we divorced I met a Dominatrix. She introduced me to a whole other life." He stopped for a moment, lost in thought. "You know, even though there are people around me all the time, I am very lonely."

"Why do you think that is?"

"There is always rejection. Things must always end."

"Rejection makes you stronger," I replied.

"I know that more than you. I am a stranger in Italy, and a stranger in America."

"You're being dramatic."

He folded his arms and smiled.

I touched his knee. "You have more friends than anyone I know. They all love you. They'll do anything you say."

"Maybe that's the problem." He took my hand. "So would you."

"No I wouldn't."

He kissed me. "You will. Lauren, I will never be well," he

said, shaking his head.

"No, you are a beautiful man." I could see through the act, but he still had some kind of hypnotic power over me. The red wine was making me feel heavy with warmth. He looked into my eyes with the pleading expression of a child. I knew that I would accept him for everything that he was.

We clung to each other and buried our faces in each other's necks. I felt that I was drowning, unable to find air, reaching up around his chest and shoulders, hoping to be reborn. Items of clothing disappeared one by one. Then Nico broke through the whirlwind and spoke.

"Lauren. I have to tell you something. I have herpes. It's nothing to worry about, I don't have an outbreak, but you should know."

"Oh," I said feeling confused. I'd never thought of this before. How susceptible was I?

"I always use condoms, there's no need to worry."

"I'm fine with it then," I said in nervous acceptance. The desire to meld with him was too strong. I honestly didn't care if it killed me. If he became a part of me, I knew I could love myself more.

"I'm very safe about it."

"Okay."

He brushed my hair from my face and his seriousness turned into a smile. We kissed, and he began the dance of arousing me so thoroughly that I cried to have him. But the tears were for Irving as well. As I navigated new foreign territory, I missed him even more.

"You are a good woman," whispered Nico, "But you have so much pain."

My fears began to dissipate and confusion fell to the back of my mind. Tears continued to stream down my face as he entered me. Nico wiped them away as my limbs stretched out. My body jolted with energy as he thrust over and over, his hands closing gently around my neck. My veins grew thick with lack of breath and energy charged out from my core down to my fingertips and toes.

"I can go for hours," he said. "I can orgasm without

ejaculation."

"Marvelous," I choked out. Our bodies glowed with sweat. Passing out in the early morning hours, we awoke at dawn for more. Afterwards we laid in bed, parallel to each other, dazed and half conscience.

"What will Irving think?" I asked.

"Who cares what Irving will think. Anyway, he's in Italy for the month."

"Yes, I suppose so. But I feel that I'm betraying him somehow. And yet, I always knew this would happen."

"You wanted it to happen. I wanted it to happen. It's a beautiful thing. If he's upset, he deserves to be."

"But I'm not doing this out of spite. I've wanted to know you more. I've wanted you. But I still love him. I miss him."

"It's okay to love him and be with me. When you love someone, it doesn't mean that you should try to claim them. You wanted to change him. But that's not love."

"I just wanted him to feel for me what I felt for him."

"But he didn't. Deal with it Lauren. Anyway, what a waste if we had never slept together! I will find you a good boy. You know, if you ever find someone, I will understand. Maybe I shouldn't find you a good boy. You have so much writing to do for the rest of your life and you don't have time for a boyfriend! You need a lover, instead."

Chapter 28

Nico attracted more women than I could count. Everywhere we went he played a game where he'd turn on the yearning orphan eyes and fawn over women like they were goddesses. Kissing them with a few words in his Italian accent and they melted immediately. He made it look so easy. And the more I watched him, the more I realized it was all an act. People are not interested in reality. They want a fantasy, an escape.

Nico the real person was often depressed, afraid of rejection, a tormented artist who was desperate to be loved and accepted by everyone. He craved power through the people that loved him.

He had no qualms about introducing me to all of the women he was involved with. There were all types - short, tall, slim, fat, old, young, glamorous, nerdy, strait-laced, or all-out fetishist. The ones that really stuck around were generally introverted and lacking in confidence. They clung to him, driven to do things they never imagined. I was one of them, of course.

There was one woman who he called his, "number one."

Her name was Jo and she labeled herself a lesbian, but Nico called himself a lesbian as well. I always felt it was a slap in the face to lesbians for him to say that, because he really did not understand women at all. He only understood how to get what he wanted from them.

Nico was the only man that Jo slept with. Which in all honesty, makes sense. Once you have been with Nico it is very hard to go back to other men, and a lot of his ex-lovers became lesbians. Few men share the sexual intensity that he had. It was like being ruined by the god Pan. How could you go back to normal humans after such a mystical encounter? With every beautiful, naïve young thing he claimed he'd found the love of his life. They came and went so quickly that it was impossible to feel threatened. From my own experience, I found that my jealousy of other women slowly turned into a sort of melding with Nico. I began to desire women as well, and once I saw things from his point of view, it no longer bothered me.

Women came around for relief from their routines to feed a primal hunger, and he fed them all, fingers dripping with juices of fruit, meat, sweat and semen. And when their knocks on the door became too persistent he would shut down and move on until they didn't care as much. But every now and then, his door would open again. Boyfriends and husbands came and went and sometimes it didn't matter if they had not gone at all.

I entered the front door of Nico's house and my energy dropped at the sight of Jo. She sat slung low and sprawling on the easy chair, her camera on the table next to her. Nico loved her strength. She never bought anything new, never wore make-up or brushed her hair. It hung scraggly around her bare face above the rumpled collar of an old flannel shirt and jeans ten years out of date. She had the slouch of an activist; too busy serving the world to care about composure. She was becoming a well-known photographer.

"Hello," I said.

"Oh, hey," responded Jo, pretending to barely notice that I'd entered the front door. Her hostile gaze belittled me, and I searched for a way out.

Nico came bounding up the stairs. "Lauren!" He ran to me, picking me up and spinning around.

"Have you met Jo?"

Jo nodded in the chair, refusing to stand up or speak. There was nothing for her to say to another sometime girl. She was above it all.

Nico and I had gone shopping earlier in the week for a Halloween party that night, but most of my get-up consisted of leftovers from the year before. I ducked downstairs to his bedroom and waited for Jo to leave. Sifting through my bag, I darkened my eyes with eyeliner and put on fishnets, hot pants, a corset, and high-heeled boots.

An hour later I sat in the living room waiting for Nico. I flipped through a book of erotic photography I'd found on the table a few weeks ago. Viewing the array of body types, I discovered a narcissistic appreciation for my own wispy physicality. Cushiony flesh somehow threatened my independence with a fear of the maternal - wrapped away in soft seclusion, sheltered obscurity, gaping cleavage sagging downwards. What little change I had gone through in adolescence had been enough for me to handle. I recalled the days when my body had become foreign to me, and I had felt nauseous with sudden awareness.

Nico's housemate Colin walked in, "You look stunning Lauren. I fancy that pair of fishnets on you."

"Thank you. I had all this from a sexy devil costume I wore last year. But I didn't want to do that again. It felt stale. So, don't know what I am this year."

"Well, you look fantastic. Obviously, I'm just dressed as myself. Think I might tag along though."

"Oh you should," I said, ducking my head back down toward the book.

"I don't know where Nico is, but he shouldn't just keep you waiting here."

"Oh, I'm fine. He's looking up directions to the party or something."

Colin drifted into the kitchen to glance through the fridge

in search of Nico's leftovers. I thought again of the proposal for a threesome, and wished my awkward shock had not gotten in the way.

Driving to the party, fog hovered over the street that glistened with fresh rain and pine needles. Pumpkins sat on every doorstep, glowering with devilish cut out eyes and crazy grins. Inside a random house, bulbs had been replaced with red lights. One woman was covered in silver sparkles, her blue eyes surrounded by rhinestones, floating as though from out of the sea. Bright colors pranced with boas, faux fur, and feathers. Nico wore a long black vinyl dress and held a leash attached to a studded collar around my neck. I stood a foot taller than him in platform boots and felt like a tall alien from a science fiction film being led by a strange little man with secrets.

It felt powerful to be with Nico, as though the world revolved around us. He made me feel wanted, beautiful, exciting, and slightly dangerous. I ceased to be average. Every night we walked into the unknown.

We sat in a dimly lit room upstairs. There were interesting looking people all around us, though none of them said anything interesting at all. I gazed around listening to empty voices, growing restless. Nico could not stay in one place for more than five minutes, and I was grateful to stand up and keep moving.

A dark gothic man with a paunch and slicked hair appeared in the hallway.

"Excuse me, will you be Lauren's master for a little while?" asked Nico. I recoiled.

"With pleasure," he replied, smiling suddenly. I felt disdain for theatrical men who used such expressions as, "With pleasure," or, "Charmed I'm sure." Nevertheless, my leash was already handed over.

"I'm not so sure about this," I said to Nico.

"Oh it will be fun. And anyway, I can't drag you around all night. I must explore!"

"My name is Steffen, what's yours?"

"Lauren."

"Come with me, I am your master now."

"Hey, nice leash," called a man dressed in orange, purple and grey.

"Thank you," I said, as I placed my hand on my hip and struck a jaunty pose.

"So what do you do?" spoke Steffen.

"I hate that question. I prefer, what do you like to do."

"So, what do you like to do?"

"I like to write, be lazy, sit by the water, have sex, watch obscure films, go to parties."

"And what do you do?" he said, laughing.

"I work as a hostess at a restaurant."

"Ah, nice. I work at Microsoft."

"The scourge of the earth."

"Don't be so harsh. Technology is the future."

"That's what you think. Technology is an oncoming breakdown. It turns people into extensions of machines."

"Well, I tried to respect what *you* do. I could have gone on a diatribe about hostess's being flighty little gold-diggers."

"I'm not really enjoying this, and I have to go to the bathroom."

"Well, you know, I can't let go of the leash. It would be disrespectful to Nico. And besides, you underestimate me and should get to know me better."

"Alright then," I said sarcastically.

"Soon computers will manage our lives. In fact, they already do to a large extent. Our thoughts uploaded to the universal consciousness, everything taken care of by the press of a button."

"I don't want that. I want simple beauty and soul. I want to struggle for things. There's no challenge in the press of a button."

Drum and bass pulsated on the floor beneath us as Steffen led me up the stairs through a stream of spinning blue lights. He caressed my arm from shoulder to wrist.

"You and I, Lauren, are just two people passing in the night. Let's leave it at that. Tonight I am your master. Have I mentioned I think you're beautiful?"

"Thank you," I said, subdued for the moment.

"You're welcome."

"And I have to go to the bathroom."

"Here we are. I'll just hold your leash and you'll go right in there."

I laughed and slid around the door, pulling my hot pants down. "This is a funny night," I called.

"It is, isn't it?" he yawned, sounding bored. I came out and he pushed his glasses up his nose.

"I wonder where Nico is?"

"Does it matter?" he asked.

"A little. He has flirting and kissing to do, and I accept that. With the last guy, I thought I could change him. But I couldn't. With Nico, I know this is the way he will always be. He needs to be constantly adored. He likes to feel he is spreading love wherever he goes. But I want to feel that I am number one."

"Come sit with me," gestured Steffen. We entered a barren room with only a couch in the middle.

"Is it dumb that I am telling you this?" I asked.

"No, not at all."

"Sometimes guys look at me funny if I talk about some other guy in their presence, as though they should be the only man in existence. How insecure."

"I'm not insecure, just a little creepy," he laughed.

"I would imagine you're also just a little rich, so you'd better watch out. I might be a gold-digger."

He cleared his throat, "Well, I never said that I would be averse to that."

"What's that little door?" I asked, pointing to the corner of the room. He stood, and gave my leash a tug. I tripped after. He pulled the knob, and found a mini-room with a vaulted ceiling. A purple glow from the party lights made his face look pale and sickly. I suddenly felt dizzy with liquor and wanted to escape.

"Come in here with me," he commanded.

My body was beginning to feel like dead weight. I laid down against the carpet. The hairs on his face stood out brittle and sparse, his rotund stomach stretched the fabric of his shirt. His burgundy velvet blazer brushed up against my arm, sticky, fuzzy and synthetic.

"Since I am your master now, you'll need to do as I say." He rolled on top of me and tried to kiss me.

"Ugh! Get off me!" I said, pushing him up. "I can handle my own leash." I grabbed the strap from his hand and dashed out of the room, leaving Steffen in a pile of velvet and purple light. I held tightly onto the leash, afraid that someone else would grasp onto it, and bounded down the stairs in my very high black boots.

Nico paraded around the living room with four girls who flailed their arms to the rhythm of the music. Stoned faces gazed across the room, red-eyed and dilated, looking half-asleep.

"Lauren, where have you been?"

"I was stuck with that techie freak. Who is he anyway?"

"I don't know. You didn't have to stay with him."

"He was nasty."

"Dance with us, Lauren."

I felt safe under his gaze, adored by someone that I could adore. He kissed me and twirled off lifting his combat boots, one after the other, looking like a broken robot. His hair flip-flopped back and forth and I laughed in relief. I could breathe again. The girls smiled at me and I began to spin.

Chapter 29

"Nothing can cure the soul but the senses,
just as nothing can cure the senses but the soul."

Oscar Wilde

In that summer before my senior year of college, one night of orgasmic pleasure with Erik changed the way I experienced everything. I always had a strong bond with nature, but now I became one with it. Life was sex. All five of my senses sprung to attention. My hands on my skin, the smell of dirt, plants, trees, air, the pain I poured into playing the piano, the emotions different colors made me feel.

Even the chemistry of my skin changed. The cutting edge perfume at the time was *Angel* – a citrus chocolate blend. When I first tried it on I loved the smell, but on my skin it sickened me into a headache. But post-virginity it blended perfectly, and everywhere I went, people loved it.

I began writing poetry to express all my new feelings - a giant binderful of them, soppy with too much feeling and not enough restraint. So naïve, but also beautiful in what I strove to express.

Eleven weeks later, Erik came back from tour. I moved into my first apartment with a roommate at the start of senior year. Though I was only twenty miles away, Erik kept putting me off. Finally, he agreed to meet in Portland for lunch. When I saw him, his face looked twisted.

"You look great!" he stammered.

He took me to a chain restaurant called, Rock Bottom. We sat down and suffered through small talk for a while. Everything seemed wrong.

"I gained ten pounds in Europe. Horrible. Too much pasta," he said.

"That's funny, I *lost* ten pounds," I replied. I compared our weight to how much I gave, and how much he took in. I looked into his eyes trying to read him.

"You're making me uncomfortable. Didn't you say before, that eye contact makes you nervous?" he asked.

"No, that wasn't me."

He looked down. "I have something to tell you that's kind of hard."

"Okay."

"Well, I've kind of gotten back together with an ex-girlfriend, Cheri. We're not just dating, we're sleeping together too."

"Oh."

Erik continued talking, but I blanked out the sound, so that all I experienced were his silent lips moving. I went to the bathroom and tried my best to hold it together. I would not allow myself to feel until we said goodbye. We walked to the Square and he showed me pictures from his travels. All I could see was how insecure and unhappy he was beneath all his claims of happiness. I was certain that he was gay and struggling to come to terms with himself. Maybe in fact, it was why I was attracted to him in the first place. He was not afraid of his feminine side.

He had to leave to see a friend he was very excited to see. He kissed both my cheeks and I started to cry. We began walking away from each other in two different directions. Then we both turned and blew kisses through the crowd. I knew I would never see him again.

I couldn't control the tears anymore. People stared at me as though I was crazy. Worse, I couldn't remember where I'd parked, what garage, what floor even. I wandered trying to find my way and walked through endless floors until I finally saw my red car.

The drive back to my apartment felt like hours. By the halfway point, I was having violent feelings toward myself. I wanted to chop off my hands. I wanted to plunge a knife into my chest. Anything to erase the emotional pain I was feeling. I got home and sat on the kitchen floor with the butcher's knife. I pressed the knife in, and let up as it stung. Small cuts crisscrossing, but never too deep.

For the next four months I cried every time I was alone. If I wasn't crying or feeling violent I was getting myself off with anything I could find – a banana, a cucumber, a flower vase, a shampoo bottle. I bought a dildo and broke it within a week. Three times a day I was getting off wherever or whenever I could.

Studying was impossible unless I was at the coffee shop surrounded by voices. I had nothing in common with the people I knew before, so I made new friends. They were all extremely social, assertive, beautiful, sexual, and daring.

I hated going to chapel. The lax deadness of the students depressed me. In crowds, I also cried. Rooms full of people made me feel too much.

Chapter 30

I wandered through a mixture of neon rooms in a dark, cavernous warehouse. Guests roamed in pajamas and negligees in homage to the latest theme, a naughty pajama party. Nico bounded towards me with a big stuffed teddy bear calling, "I won the cock ring toss!" He promptly handed me the bear and lifted me over his shoulder, spinning wildly.

"Put me down!" I laughed as my short black skirt rode up to my waist.

He set me down and danced off in his tight tube dress and combat boots, jumping up and down. I felt lost without him right next to me, because not far away, Irving was seeking attention. I hadn't expected him to be there and it was unnerving to be in the same room with him. He had spread rumors that I was using his friends to stalk him. He didn't like that I went salsa dancing with his friend George, and most of all that I was sleeping with one of his closest friends. It didn't look good from his point of view. But I had no choice. Nico was magnetic.

In one swooping motion, Irving grabbed my hand from behind and spun me toward him. I remembered the first time we had danced and how he failed to lead. But now it didn't matter, because I had a sense of control. He pulled his moves, gazing out from underneath upturned brows, as though he had studied his expressions in the mirror. I smiled at him aware that it was all for the benefit of those watching. I was available and able to make him appear more intriguing.

"I don't know sweetheart. Two nights in a row," he said, referring to a brief run-in at salsa night, the evening before. I hadn't known that he was back from Europe yet, otherwise, I would have avoided the ballroom altogether.

"Looks like you're stalking me," I retorted.

The song ended, he let me go, and I went spinning across the floor. I found myself in front of Nico.

"You should be avoiding him. Don't feed his ego."

"I didn't have much of a choice. And I do kind of miss him."

"Just stay away from him. If you ever sleep with Irving again I will never have sex with you again. Don't mess things up!"

"Whatever," I said, walking off. A beautiful boy in a purple pajama top approached me.

"Hello."

"Hi."

"May I kiss you?"

"Yes." His lips touched mine. We smiled at each other and kissed again. I turned and drifted over to the kissing booth where an older woman with long curly hair smiled out at me.

"Aren't you Nico's friend?" she asked.

"Oh? Oh yes, you're Jo. I remember now." I sensed an oncoming threat.

"You know. He has so many diversions."

"And I'm fully aware that I'm one of them!" I laughed. Jo squinted down at me.

"Would you like to purchase a kiss? The money goes to the arts."

"No thank you. I'm broke," I said, as I shrugged my shoulders and walked away. Two old men approached like relics from the era of free love. One poked his tongue through the gap between his two front teeth. "If you're ever in need, I have special talents," he said. His friend laughed lasciviously.

"My needs are definitely taken care of," I laughed.

Nico reappeared with the teddy bear. "Kiss the bear Lauren, kiss the bear!"

"I don't want to kiss the bear. I'm sure everyone else has!"

"Just kiss the bear."

I kissed it on the nose.

"That bear is a total ho! I can't believe you just kissed it!" yelled an obnoxious girl.

Nico glared at her.

"I saw Jo at the kissing booth," I said.

"Ah yes, my girlfriend. But tonight she has a date, that blonde woman over there. So I'm trying to stay away. Her date might end up wanting *me* instead."

"Yes, because everyone does," I winked.

We all tumbled out of the warehouse and congregated in the street. Nico appeared, followed by Irving and his friend Ilan from Florida. A cop drove by, amused by the creatures lurking over cobblestones. He spoke over the intercom to Nico, "Put on some clothes!"

Nico turned about face, "I'm a woman! I'm a woman!"

"Yeah, a woman with a twelve inch dick!"

"That's my labia, man!"

The cop started laughing. "Everyone clear out," he boomed as he slowly drove away.

"You must take Ilan home with you," spoke Irving. "He's allergic to my cats."

We all piled into cars, and Ilan stumbled into the backseat behind Nico and I. His boyish eyes pranced over my thighs. At the house Ilan kept trying to push me into empty rooms, hands wandering across my body. But over and over I dodged out of his grasp until I was in bed with Nico, Ilan disposed of in the guest room.

Chapter 31

A few days later Nico and I entered a hazy red-lit room
that looked like an opium den. Sweat broke out on the brows
of everyone present. The heat was turned up too high and it
felt as though we were in a jungle. Dolmas and nectarines
were passed around in Chinese rice bowls. Mattresses were
spread across the floor beneath long rectangles of fabric
reaching to tacks stuck in the low ceiling. It was a small get-
together, hosted by Nico's friend Nuri.

Nuri's eyes were piercing beneath two arched brows.
Sitting on the floor with his arm resting on a knee, he turned
to us and said, "This woman approached me at the Vogue. She
wasn't wearing anything eye-catching, just everything black. I
was sitting at the bar, and she sat down next to me. 'Take me
home with you,' she said. 'Do whatever you like to me. I want
to be dominated. I'm so tired of dominating everyone at work;
I need someone to control me. Please.'"

"So what did you say to her?" I asked.

"I said, 'Of course.'" He looked me directly in the eye and
smiled slyly. I swallowed.

Nico jumped up, "It's hot in here. I can't take it

anymore!" He crossed his arms and reached for the hem of his shirt, pulling it up and over his head, his pants coming down afterwards. He sat back, naked, except for his socks. All ten guests perked up from their stupor.

"We should have a photo shoot," said the dark woman in the corner, taking a bite from a nectarine. She was an editor at an art magazine.

"Excellent idea!"

A camera appeared and everyone took turns recording their interpretations of Nico's naked body leaning across mattresses strewn with roses and cloves. I placed a long branch of eucalyptus along his spine representing his vertebrae. One man asked me to lie across Nico, fully clothed.

"We would love to photograph you making love."

"No, that's okay," I said, waving my hand, "I don't want to."

"It would be beautiful."

"Not in the mood for that. I guess I like the art of this. But I'm not feeling pornography."

"Oh come on."

I loved the dynamic of the male being objectified while the woman remained fully clothed, the opposite of classical art. Nico smiled at me with an expression I hadn't seen before. I took his hand, as he laid stomach-down on the mattress. The angles of his face glowed in the candlelight. Everyone seemed excruciatingly bored, as though the further you inched to the edge of a cliff the more unbearable it was not to jump over. The entire party dissipated with my lame answer. But I didn't care. These people were all strangers to me. I was a nomad passing through, drifting in and out of gatherings, absorbing people and places until I could finally fall into Nico's bed for the satisfaction of my sexual fix.

Nico put his clothes back on and we exited out the back door.

"Ugh! It was so hot in there! I couldn't stand it!" he exclaimed. His spirits were high and I felt lucky to finally be alone with him.

"I really have to piss," he said.

"Well, why didn't you go inside?"

"Too late now," he stated, unzipping his pants. He peed against the high brick foundation of the house, "L-A-U-R-E-N! It's so wonderful to just pee your name on walls!"

We laughed and then drove to his house. In his bedroom I took in the smells and objects that had become so familiar. The mysterious cat lady painting, the creeping philodendrons against red walls, and the old wheelchair in the corner, musty with mortality. I sat on the swing and Nico kneeled below me, kissing my waist, moving over crevices and angles. Soon my stomach was resting on the swing and I felt like a swan, flying through the air, landing over and over on his prick. Somehow he never missed with each landing.

Eventually I turned and we were on the bed. He was reaching up, it seemed right through my center. I wanted to open wider and wider, to split apart completely.

"Baby, I'm fisting you."

I didn't believe him and looked down where his fist had disappeared. "It feels so good," I gasped, surprised that my body could offer up so much to him. And still I was starving for more. I wondered if I could ever be satiated. The hunger was excruciating, and it didn't feel like love. It felt like an addiction.

Chapter 32

I was sitting in biology class, senior year, so bored I thought my eyeballs would melt. I began to fantasize that a gun was blowing away every limb of my body. I could feel every excruciating bullet zip through my skin. The lead was poisoning my veins, and my own destruction felt so good. I envisioned myself pulling the trigger to my head. The boom blasted inside my brain.

But maybe first, I could use the house key that Erik had dropped on the floor of my car to sneak into his house in the middle of the night. I would creep up the stairs and find him in bed with Cheri. Flipping the switch, their shocked faces could take me in, standing there with a gun. They would huddle naked beneath the white sheets that would soon be stained with their blood. I desperately wanted a gun. I wanted power over a situation that made me feel completely helpless. I had no say. I had nothing but all of these overwhelming emotions and hundreds of bad poems.

After class, instead of going home to sit on the kitchen floor with the butcher's knife pressed to my wrist, I went to the counselor's office. The counselor wasn't there. An over-friendly nurse sat me down in the waiting room.

"So I just need to ask you some questions," she said with her best sympathetic smile. She had the bulbous eyes of a goldfish. "What brings you in here today?"

I felt shaky and embarrassed to say why I was there. "I feel like I'm going to hurt myself."

"Oh. Okay. I'm sorry to hear that." She looked away, suddenly avoiding eye contact, then wrote something down on her clipboard.

I had just admitted that I wanted to commit a sin.

"I'll be right back." She stood up and walked through the white door. I peered through the long rectangular window in the door and watched as she disappeared into a room. I stared down at the flat grey carpet, fighting the instinct to bolt. Just as I was about to make my move, she reappeared with a practiced expression of sadness.

She held a piece of paper out to me. "I don't exactly know what the normal procedure is, but this always makes me feel better."

I took the paper. The heading read, "One Hundred Things That Make Me Happy." The list included things like ice cream cones, bubbles, and the beach. I was surprised to see that unicorns were not on the list. I suddenly felt like I was in kindergarten. My complex problems had just been simplified into a bunch of fluff. Poof! You can blow them away with the happy thought of bubbles! But watch how quickly they pop. Watch how that ice cream cone can make you fat. Watch how the waves at the beach can pull you under.

"I would like to set you up with sessions to see one of our student counselors. They are in the masters program, but you'll see, they're very good. Before you leave today, you'll need to sign this contract," she said, handing it to me.

I read it through. The contract said that I would not hurt

myself. If I felt the desire was too much, I was to call a list of four contacts. The list included a parent, a friend, the counselor's office, or 911. I wondered what would happen if I broke the contract. If my suicide were not a success, would they punish me?

I left the office, and realized that somehow, signing the contract had helped me. I didn't feel quite as alone as before. The impulse was still there, and I still cried everyday for months, especially in crowds, especially in chapel. But I came to understand that it was all a part of the process. The knives, the gun fantasies, the need for physical pain seemed like a relief from all the emotional pain.

But beyond that, I was killing off the side of myself that needed to die. The person I was told to be, I never was. Happiness was somewhere on the other side. And it didn't involve ice cream cones, bubbles, or even the beach.

Chapter 33

"I had loved her with the fury of my ego...
but I loved her the way a drum majorette loved
the power of the band
for the swell it gave to each little strut."

Norman Mailer

I sat at the table watching Nico cook. He shook clams in a large pot with butter and wine, and then flipped the sautéed spinach. I sipped my red wine. "You know that guy that led me around on the leash called me the other night," I said.

"Oh really?"

"I have no idea how he got my phone number. Do you know by any chance?"

"I didn't give it to him."

"He's creepy. He kept saying my name. I didn't know who it was at first. He tried to have sex with me in the closet at that party. I didn't find him at all attractive."

"You know, you should see other people besides just me," Nico said.

"If I find someone worth seeing, I will. Quality over

quantity."

"It's not healthy. I don't want you to depend on me. You know I will never change. I love many, many people. I will never be faithful to one person only. I am faithful to all the people I love."

"I haven't asked you to change. And why should I look elsewhere when you satisfy me?" I asked.

"It's not an open relationship unless we are both open."

"I'm not interested in anyone else."

"Sometimes I think of being celibate. What would that be like?" Nico wondered.

"Strange. Come on. You will never be celibate. You just want to make me feel I could lose you somehow, to make me want you more."

"Oh! So now I'm playing tricks. I'm just saying, so maybe I'm a little extreme sexually. What would the opposite of that be? I don't think I could be happy without variety."

"Well. Who knows," I said, not knowing how to respond.

I didn't want a committed relationship from Nico, but I wanted to feel that I was more important to him than the other women. To climb the list, and be the one human being he could confide with, bound with him and known. He sat down at the table with two plates piled high with clams, greens, and bruschetta. I nibbled and flipped through pictures of Nico's recent trip to Italy. He pointed out family members. His siblings barely resembled him at all. I turned the page to reveal a stern looking man with glassy blue eyes set against dark leathery skin. His thin lips formed a straight line that had no curve at all.

"That is my father," Nico said.

I studied the face in the photograph. When I looked up, Nico's face was streamed with tears. He was lost in the past.

"He is a hard worker. We could never be just kids. Always working like slaves on the farm. I hated him. I hated the way he treated my mother."

I sucked on a clam, and then crunched down on the bruschetta. "The clams are very good," I said, uncomfortably.

"They are easier to make than most people think."

I smiled. The silence between us made my lungs feel empty.

Later we went downstairs and watched an obscure Japanese porn film. A lecherous patriarch ran around his house assaulting all sorts of women. He snuck up behind an obese housemaid and attacked. Her buttocks rippled with force as the man made gruesome faces.

Nico turned out the light, and began to pretend that I was a child. He kept telling me that I needed to be punished, and I kept asking for more. He made me feel angry and tired of my young age. I wanted him to come to me without a role to play, without props, without manipulations. I wondered why life had to be so complicated. He held my hands behind my head and slapped my face. I smiled, slithered free, and flipped him over onto his back.

It was the first time he didn't use a condom with me. Nico had told me he never used one with the woman who was his number one. Jo was upset when she found out. He'd been sleeping with her unprotected for years. I felt a twisted victory, all the while knowing how stupid it was to feel that way.

. . .

I awoke to the smell of mushrooms sizzling on a skillet. Rubbing layers of sleep from my eyes, I rolled over and into the jeans I had worn the night before.

"Nico!"

"Come on up! I'm making you an omelet!" he called down the stairs.

I trudged up and into the kitchen, taking my seat at the table.

"You were sleeping so deeply, I woke up at eight, and went to the graveyard to hunt for mushrooms. I picked twenty pounds! Look at all of them!"

I surveyed the table, now covered with baskets of fungi. "You picked mushrooms this morning for my omelet?" I asked, incredulously.

"These cost a fortune. I can't believe my luck," he said, folding the omelet into a crescent and flipping it. When it was done, he slid it onto the plate delicately, next to crostini and heirloom tomatoes. He set it down in front of me and I began to eat. I was too hungry to care about corpses lying beneath where the mushrooms had grown.

"No time to shower today, we have a million things we must do, friends that need food and visits, the world is calling, Lauren!" he exclaimed, slapping his chest. I laughed.

Still waiting an hour later, I bemoaned the fact that I'd had plenty of time to take a shower. Nico emerged from the shed with his old white Vespa. He cursed loudly when it wouldn't start. He grabbed it by the handles and ran down the street until finally it sputtered and coughed, whirring like an overgrown wasp. He handed me an extra helmet, strapped on his old fashioned goggles, and clicked the helmet tight onto his head, adjusting the chinstrap. Then he helped adjust mine.

"Wait here while I get the food!" he yelled over the loud engine, dashing away through a thick cloud of exhaust. I stood staring at the chugging scooter as the cold chill of November seeped through my thin blazer. Nico came stumbling down the stairs in his combat boots, carrying a giant pot of soup with fresh loaves of bread. He strapped them down in the crate on the back and mounted the seat.

I swung on behind him and buried my hands deep within his purple King Lear faux fur coat. Buzzing down the street, Nico honked and waved to every pedestrian as though we were in a parade. At first I was embarrassed, but Nico's flamboyant energy was contagious, and the cold rush of air was extremely invigorating. It felt as though we were flying along, and I couldn't stop myself from yelping with joy as we turned corners and rode up steep hills. He tossed words back at me that were undecipherable yet exciting to hear. I laughed breathlessly, burying my arms deeper within the furriness of the plush coat.

Turning a bend, the lid on the soup rattled and blew up

into the air. With quick swiftness, I freed my hand and caught it behind me. We pulled over to tie it down, and took off again.

Parking on neighborhood sidewalks, Nico delivered the food, excitedly talking with friends. I stood in the background, quietly watching, absorbing the charisma he had over so many different people. He tried out a new mother's breast pump, stroked an exotic pheasant at a belly dancer's commune, and listened to his heavily tatted friend talk about an abusive ex-girlfriend.

"I have something to show you," he said to me as we sped off. "The hugest tomato plants you've ever seen!" Speeding around corners, we leaned into the brisk air that gusted against our faces. Nico's coat was covered with tiny droplets of dew.

"Tomatoes in November?"

"Seriously."

We drove around a bend where a house was literally overtaken by tomato vines. The plants towered above the house with more tomatoes than one family could possibly eat; plum tomatoes, green and orange, with big red ones weighing down the vines, heavy and bursting. Nico parked the Vespa. I breathed in with awe as he took out a few bags.

"What are you doing?"

"Picking tomatoes! We can't let these go to waste. But first I'll knock."

"You're crazy!" I was nervous about how the owners would react, failing to remember Nico's persuasiveness.

He knocked on the door. No answer. Finally a middle-aged man who looked as though he'd been taking a nap appeared. He scratched his balding head at the sight of Nico in the King Lear coat with wild hair sticking straight out from the goggles pushed up on his forehead. Then he looked over at me and smiled.

"We wanted to ask if we could pick some tomatoes. You couldn't possibly eat all these."

"Well, sure I guess. Most of them rot every year and we can't keep up with the plants."

"Do you have a secret?"

"Oh no. They grow like crazy every year. It might be the way the sun hits the brick house and heats it all up."

We walked around and picked the tomatoes, putting them in bags.

"I have to be honest with you. I actually picked some of your tomatoes before. I couldn't help myself."

The man smiled, "You know. Feel free to come back and take some more."

"They're delicious," Nico said, biting into a bright orange oval one.

I laughed over his fearlessness at admitting he was hopping gardens, stealing produce.

"Are you both from Italy?" the man asked, reminding me of how quiet I was.

"Oh no. She's American. But I am from the heel of the boot. You know, there's no freedom there. In America, I am a free man," Nico said, sticking his chest out.

"I grew up here," I piped up. The man smiled again, amused by the unexpected entertainment.

We drove home and Nico arranged tomatoes in the middle of a carving I had picked out for him at the Fremont flea market - five wooden men in a circle united by their connected arms. It appeared that they were worshipping the harvest.

Nico fed me tomatoes as I sat on the counter. He lifted up my black skirt and slipped his fingers up into me, wet and ripe. I buried my lips into his neck and he grasped my waist, firmly pressing against me. I gasped. A tomato rolled across the counter.

Chapter 34

I was hanging out with Tony. We went back to Club Medusa since he'd scored some tickets for free drinks from a client. I didn't realize it was a benefit party for season-pass ticket holders of the opera. Once again, there was Irving. I could never get away from him, even when I was avoiding his scene. I knew he would gossip to Nico about how I was stalking him. I pretended not to see him, but he kept flashing me looks. Inevitably, he would come over and say something cheesy, like, "Fancy meeting you here, darling."

Irving walked over, "Well, hello you two! Where's your leash?" he asked, turning to me. "Does Nico, know you're here? I'm not sure this would be okay with him! I think I have to call him to check and find out!" He wavered on his feet and began paging through the contacts on his cell phone. He put the phone up to his ear.

"Nico! You're not going to believe who's here with another guy... Lauren! Yes! Haha!"

"You asshole," I said under my breath.

He snapped his phone closed. "Well, great to see you both, but I was just on my way out." He grabbed Tony by the shoulders and kissed him right on the lips.

"Irving!"

"Always good to see you darling," he said, kissing me as well.

Tony and I darted into the back room. We stood sipping cocktails on the side of the dance floor.

"See anyone you like?" Tony asked.

"That guy over there looks dashing. Not the sort at all I've been around lately." I pointed to a tall man in glasses and a suit. Despite the man's conservative appearance, he had the look of a sensitive poet underneath.

"How about you?" I asked.

"Nah, the women here look boring. That Irving is such a sleaze, I can't believe you dated him."

"I can't believe he was here again. He always gets season tickets to the Opera."

"The many faces of Irving."

"He can't handle running into me. He always has to do some fake shit to try and impress me."

"I'm going to ask that guy if he'd like to dance with you. He might think we're together, and if I ask, it will give him the go-ahead."

"Oh don't!"

"No, I am. He looks nice, as opposed to types like Irving and Nico."

"Oh, they're fine," I said, waving my hand.

"No really."

He walked over to the tall man who started to look nervously in my direction. Tony came back and said, "I'd like to introduce you."

"Oh god."

The rest of the evening I danced awkwardly with Brian. He was shy, but calming. I gave him my phone number and he said he'd like to take me out on Tuesday. When I left that night, I checked my phone and found an angry voicemail from Nico, thinking that I was out with Irving. When I called him back, he reported that Irving had called him again to say, "She was looking at me with those sad puppy dog eyes, so hot over me."

Nico had replied, "Get over it! She's in love with me now!" I just wanted them to grow up and stop competing with each other.

On Tuesday, my car got towed at 3pm. I had been at my modeling agency, and lost track of time. It was the type of scam agency where the employees take all the best jobs for themselves, and then called us to work for free. My parents were out of town, so Nico came and picked me up.

"You can stay at my house tonight, but you should know that I have a date with another woman."

"Well, that's okay, because I have a date with another man."

He turned and looked at me, incredulous.

"I suppose it will be a little funny having him pick me up at your house."

He laughed.

After he left, I sat waiting for 7pm. Brian arrived, and I told him I was staying at a friend's house.

"This is some place!" he exclaimed. "Look at these crazy pictures on the fridge!"

"Yeah, my friend is a little crazy. Lets get going," I said, pushing him out the door as though one more second in this house would spoil his wholesomeness forever.

Throughout the entire date I felt terrible. Brian didn't stand a chance. I was wasting his time, trying to be interested in someone who could actually be good to me. His words drifted past my ears, and I could only think of Nico, wanting him desperately, more than before. With his good clean looks, Brian was the shining example of the perfect future husband. I felt cozy there with him. There was no sign of danger, nothing to ease the lethargic comfort. I was in withdrawal.

When he dropped me off back at Nico's house, Nico was already in bed. The house was dark and cold. I crept down the stairs and slowly opened the door to his room. I was almost afraid that he would be with another woman. But he came bounding from the bed, "Lauren, I couldn't wait to be with you!"

"I know! I was dying for the whole thing to be over with!"

His arms wound tightly around me. I laid on the bed, and he undressed me slowly. He turned me stomach down on the bed and tied my arms behind me. He placed a blindfold across my eyes and tied my ankles spread apart. Feathers ran down my back and I giggled. The straps of a whip brushed across me with a slight chill. He slapped them down lightly, and then a little harder. At first I didn't cringe, but then the more I anticipated the smack, the more I feared it. I jumped with anxiety.

"I don't like this anymore, Nico."

"You don't like it? No you like to be in charge. But with me, you are not. Tonight, I am the master."

Nevertheless, he untied the black tape from my wrists and ankles and removed the blindfold. "You might like these," he said, pulling from his chest of tricks two clamps connected by a chain. He attached them to my nipples and immediately I felt charged. He brought out a plug and slowly smoothed it into me, then slid himself in as well. He brushed his thumb across my lips and I began sucking it and rolling with his rhythm.

We kept at it for hours until we were red and raw with pain. Covered in bruises with broken blood vessels that lasted for days. It felt toxic and wonderful, dangerous and alive, aware that my obsession could take me from being alive to one day feeling completely dead.

. . .

A few days later at Nico's house, I sat upstairs rocking back and forth on the couch surrounded by darkness. The shadows cast by streetlights outside, made the room appear ominous and strange. The harvestmen on the table now seemed sinister.

Earlier, Nico had shown me erotic pictures. In the photos, he was lying stomach down as his friend, Kara, hovered behind him with a strap-on. She was the one who was supposedly a showgirl in Vegas, but I didn't buy that for a minute. I hadn't wanted to see the photos, but he was so proud, he showed them to me anyway. I shivered at the images flashing through my head, but as I thought of leaving, it was more apparent that I had to go back to bed. Walking down the stairs, I entered the room. Nico sat up straight as a rod.

"I thought you had left me! That stupid body pillow, I thought it was you!" He grasped onto my waist and pulled me down onto the bed.

"I was mad at you for showing me those pictures."

"What is there to be mad about? The thought of Kara makes me go limp."

"Really?"

"We dated years ago. I could never be with her now. She's like my sister."

"That's what they all say."

He wrapped his arms around my bare limbs and held me tight to his body. I could feel his heart beating through his chest. His stomach expanded in and out with his breath against my own. I felt safe and lost at the same time. Tomorrow he would need someone else to fill in the gaps I had left behind.

In the morning, he left for English class and I dosed in and out, feeling sullen whenever I awoke. The ceiling vaulted above me and the massive philodendron curled its leafy claws along twine stretching out in all directions. The swing hung still in silence.

"Why do the men I date always have flat pillows?" I wondered out loud. I punched it, and folded it in half, a sure sign of a dead pillow. Then I remembered Erik, my first love, with his white fluffy pillows and billowing curtains. "I just *know* that Erik is gay," I surmised. Every time I said it, the rejection seemed less painful. The one rejection that seemed like it would never go away.

I looked over in the mirror on the back of the door, half shrouded by whips and feathers. My golden hair glowed like a trophy or like strength. Tony had dyed it platinum blonde. I enjoyed looking otherworldly and apart, not able even, to recognize myself in the mirror. Nico didn't like it. I pulled the covers over my head to hide the image I did not feel, and tried to fade away. Light crept in through the cracks.

Chapter 35

My roommate in my senior year was over-weight and had the firm belief that if she was thin she would look like a supermodel, and every guy would want her. But it was obvious she would still be the same person, thin or large.

Her food consisted of freezer box fare chock full of preservatives and sodium – Pizza Poppers, Hot Pockets. In the morning she ate a mixer-size bowl of Lucky Charms. I wanted to give her a nutritional makeover, but I didn't want to be rude. In the case of roommates, I tended to keep my distance to avoid conflict.

One time my friend Richard came over, and stared at her bookshelf covered with photos, diet books, and ceramic frogs. "Your roommate hates you, doesn't she?" he asked, though he already knew the answer.

"Maybe."

It was true that she was often envious of my life. She seemed to think that if people liked Lauren, people would like her too if she was more like me. She began to use the same products that I did. She told me that she wanted to buy classy clothes because she was jealous of my closet, so she got a job.

She complained that her side of the fridge was generic, while mine was healthy. I felt like I was living in the movie *Single White Female*. I just wanted her to find self-acceptance.

Sometimes she would talk to me for hours about issues with her self-image and a guy she liked who only thought of her as a friend. She was amused by all of my exploits, but disturbed by the way I was gathering sexual experience like a collector.

"A woman is a rose," she said. "Her love is the petals. She gives a petal to each man, and if there are too many men, soon the petals will all be gone, and there will be no more love to give."

"But a rose is a perennial!" I burst out. "It comes back every year. Do you really believe that love is so limited? Love is endless, the more we love, the more it grows."

Lynn had all sorts of philosophies on life. Some of them were more misguided than others.

"Can you curl your tongue?" she asked, showing me her adept tongue curl. "People who don't have the tongue-curling gene can't French kiss properly," she stated, as though it were scientific fact.

"How would you know? You've never even French kissed anyone!"

"It's true. You'll never get to experience what I will!" she exclaimed.

"You're so full of it."

She had studied all sorts of ways to perceive people in her acting classes. She studied faces in photographs and could tell me if they were dishonest or uncertain of their life choices. We looked at a photo of our previous roommate Melanie, from the suite we lived in, junior year. Melanie had just gotten married that last summer.

"Do you see this photo from when Melanie was engaged? Her face is off balance. She's not sure if she is making the right choice by getting married. But here in this photo of her after they got married, her face is in balance again. She knows she is on the right path.

"I can also tell what drives a person by how they walk.

People who walk with their head furthest forward are driven by the mind. They are very cerebral. People that walk with their chest out, are driven by their heart. Maybe that's why guys like girls with big boobs."

"Whatever."

"People who walk with their pelvis forwards are driven by sex. You are most certainly driven by your pelvis."

I laughed.

Chapter 36

"I don't love people I can dominate."

Colette

At the Vogue nightclub, a stale stench of sweat, urine, and spilt liquor made the air feel dense. Black walls and curtains made the room seem larger than it was. A lanky man in hot pants and a boa danced around a pole. His muscles glistened under the strobe lights as he thrust and swayed to the repetitive beat of industrial music. The pulsing bass was overlaid with rhythmic whips slapping down on a treble beat.

A woman with cropped bangs strode past the dancer as though she were on a catwalk, wearing only fishnets, a black thong and two pieces of black tape that covered her nipples. I tried my best not to stare, though I was completely enamored. I stood watching behind a high rectangular table that surrounded the dance floor. I wore hot pants, a black woven bikini with fringe, fishnets and six-inch platform peep-toe heels.

When we had arrived, Nico bought me a Long Island and disappeared. I could see him now, not far off, talking to a woman. She fondled his arm and flashed her eyes at him with her fat cheeks bulging as much as her breasts. I mused over Nico in his tight spandex tube dress and combat boots, and smiled over how the feminine attire enhanced his masculinity.

A bear of a man walked past me and grasped Nico by the arms, kissing him forcefully. Nico tensed up and shrank back. The man said something I couldn't hear. Then Nico dodged away, and swooped over to me. It was the first time I ever saw him without control over a situation.

"How does the basil I put in your little pants feel?" he asked me.

"Refreshing. You could start a trend and call it herbs in undies. Enhance your natural flavors."

"That's my girl," he said, slapping my ass. I put my hand on my hip and pursed my lips at him.

"Listen," he said, "I have someone I want you to meet. He likes to be beaten and goes by the name Community Carl. He needs to be put in his place. I want you to dominate him."

"I'm not sure I can handle that."

"Of course you can! I'll teach you! He'll love it. You're just the sort he likes."

Nico took my hand, and I tottered behind in the very tall shoes. He was like a crazy little elf guiding me to the netherworld. We came to the back of the club where a doorway was covered with black curtains. I was afraid to enter. Who knew what was going on behind. Nico pulled the curtain aside and guided me in where an older man with a mustache was tied to the wall by his wrists. His shirt was off, and he seemed like a remnant from an old porno film. His bare chest was leathery, gravity pulling his skin down crease by crease.

"Please, I need to be beaten," Carl begged, head hanging down towards the floor.

Nico abruptly slapped him in the face, "Does that feel good?"

"I need more. I want it to hurt."

"Lauren he's begging for it. You can do whatever you want to him. You can twist his nipples, slap him, or punch him. Just don't hit his kidneys in the lower back, here and here," he instructed, placing his hands across the sway of the man's back. "Any damage to the kidneys could be fatal. But the rest is yours."

"Okay," I said, hesitating as I stared at Community Carl.

"You can do anything you want to him."

"I need to be beaten down," whimpered Carl. I whaled into his chest with my fist, and my strength surprised me.

"Oh fuck!" he yelped.

I whacked his thigh then twisted his left nipple tight between my fingers.

"Good girl, Lauren," said Nico, as though I were an obedient canine. "You just keep at it, and I'll be back soon," he said, patting my shoulder.

I looked at Nico with a touch of panic, but after his exit, my aggression turned on Carl. A man handed me a crop and I whipped Carl back and forth across his stomach and chest. His face pinched in pain and he sucked in air with each sting of black leather. He twisted and flailed against the wall. I hated that Nico always left me. What was he doing? Why did he need so much attention?

Carl looked gruesome in his pseudo submissive state. I could see beneath his act that he had spent a lifetime on a ruthless treadmill of self-importance. Physical pain seeped through his body, erasing the emptiness of his emotions. All the things he had believed in at a young age eventually became a lie. Blood vessels bulged in his neck as he cringed. He wanted it all to be beaten out of him. The crop in my hand zipped through the air and came down on his skin with a loud whap.

His eyes rolled back into his head as he whimpered, "I need more."

"Do you?" I whacked him once more across the thigh. An audience had gathered at the door. I felt taken up into another existence. The vinyl had been a costume for me, but now my appearance was being interpreted as fact. I surveyed all the people watching the role that had gone past pretend. My mind was a cloud of manufactured fog and neon beams of light flipping to the consistent sounds of a lash.

Nico came bursting through the curtains, "Lauren! Don't you think you're getting carried away?"

"Not at all," I replied, whacking Carl again.

"Come with me."

"No."

"Yes!" Nico commanded, taking my hand. "I want you to meet a man. He's very rich. He could be good for you!" he spit into my ear, over the loud music. "You could live on your own. He could set you up."

"I don't want to meet anyone else. I've found you, haven't I?"

"No, you *must* meet Franco. He's been asking about you."

Nico led me out to the bar where a rotund man in a bow tie sat. He looked like an opera singer.

"Franco! This is Lauren. She's quite good with a whip."

Franco laughed jovially as I held out my hand. He kissed it while I distractedly sipped my Long Island.

"The pleasure is all mine," he said.

"I didn't know people used phrases like that anymore," I replied.

"You have a beautiful smile. You know you are going to make an amazing mother with a smile like that," mused Franco.

"A mother?" My eyebrows creased together in confusion.

"Some little boy will be raised well because you exist in this world. You're a rich woman, and any boy would love to have a mother like you. Easygoing and artistic, I can tell," he added.

"You are a strange bird," I said, laughing. "A strange, strange bird." I shook my head.

Maybe Franco had a mother fetish, but I certainly wasn't the motherly type. Nico told me I had the body of an adolescent boy. I began to shimmy and moved backwards, edging away from the two men who suddenly seemed foreign and strange and faraway. They watched me move as I closed my eyes and ate up their stares. I traveled into another dimension, beyond the creatures that circled like extras from a sci-fi film. I was a voyeur of my own life.

. . .

It was the time of year when the season turns grey and
brisk with crystals of frost that form before dawn. I closed
Nico's red front door gently behind me and walked past the
strangely configured broken white reproduction statues from
various sites in Rome. Exiting the wind-torn curtains
obscuring the entrance to the porch, I walked down the stairs.
I breathed in, and the thick wet air seeped into my nostrils.
Turning the key in the lock, I stepped into my aging hand-me-
down car. The transmission was dying due to the time it was
towed in second gear.

I felt poetic, nostalgic, and pure, like a virgin ready to be
sacrificed to Dionysian delights or death itself. I turned down
the street and drove through slumbering neighborhoods. The
whole world seemed to be drowsy with hibernation. But
amidst all the deadness I felt so awake.

My long monotonous shift at work would have little
meaning in the knowledge that I was living an extraordinary
life. I took risks that my friends would never dream of. I
couldn't care less about protecting my emotions if it meant it
would hold me back from really living. But I wanted the
parallel life to stop. I was tired of all the people from my past
that shook their heads over things they didn't understand.
Though I loved them, there was nothing between us anymore.
And I hated regressing back into the Lauren I had left behind,
the one who faked everything just to be accepted. Then I
thought of the costume I had worn the night before, and
realized, that too was an act.

Chapter 37

I sat by Lake Washington, on a bench under a willow tree. It was New Years Eve and I was alone. Nico was in the midst of his own party and told me I couldn't go because he already had two dates. But I had to work that night anyway, and got off only a half hour before midnight. I was in excruciating pain.

Earlier that week we had been obsessive in our hunger for each other. He'd been less than careful, leaving my body raw with a Urinary Tract Infection. The next day I had a fever and felt weak. In the shower I felt a strange bump along the right side of my labia. It stung as I touched it. Within hours the painful bumps multiplied and I panicked over the loss of control over my body. They grew in lesions, even on my thumb and all down my throat so that I could barely swallow. Like needles pricking all through me, it was painful to sit, painful to stand, painful to lie down. I silently cried through the sting at Christmas dinner, but I still wouldn't tell anyone what was wrong.

Two days later the doctor was shocked by the extreme case of herpes. She brought in an Intern to observe, as though

I was some kind of freak show in our small suburban town. The doctor turned from her file and said flatly, "The man that did this to you should be punished." She sent me home with some very expensive pills that I could not really afford.

My mind raced constantly with fear that my entire body could be overtaken, the disease multiplying out of control. I scrutinized every inch of my skin to make certain the lesions were not still growing, shocked at the way my body was failing me for the very first time.

Soon after, I went to Nico's house, angry over my own weakness. He had told me the truth in the beginning and I still didn't want to have protected sex. I had cared less about my own wellbeing than for being his number one. My competitiveness disgusted me. And now I was strangely united with him in our shared pain. He held me and we both cried. Sexually, I could see my value slipping off the pedestal. My body was now the enemy. I wanted to have distance from my physical self and the impulses that sprung out of control.

The clock struck midnight. Across the water fireworks burst into the black night creating the shapes of my own scars. Along the street behind me people crowded onto balconies and cheered loudly. In that moment, my strength began crushing the weakness of my body. I began to cry over the beauty of being alone with no one to distract me from all that I could feel. The worst part of being with people was pretending that nothing was wrong. I wrote down some resolutions in my journal, including, "I will feel less next year." Turning inwards and away from all that could push and pull my emotions into an unbearable knot.

Chapter 38

"God did not create man in his own image.
Evidently it was the other way about..."

Christopher Hitchens

When I was twenty-one, my sister didn't give up on me without a fight. When she read I was slipping, she wrote to me from her mission base in Papua New Guinea that I should go to some place in Texas for nine months of discipleship training. Her other idea was that I live with a Christian family on Whidbey Island, start serving at their Assemblies of God church, and be assigned someone to disciple me daily.

"There are so many things about 'Christianity' that I never learned at home, because we, in general as a family, don't talk much about what is going on inside, spiritually and emotionally," she wrote.

After going to Christian schools all the way through college, I knew the books of the Bible and what they involved like the back of my hand. My mother was offended when she saw the letter. "I read you Bible stories every night growing up! And I don't want you going to that church of theirs. That pastor is too condemning and legalistic. You don't need all of that. It wouldn't be right for you."

My mom was right. She was the only one not trying to push me into something. I wanted to please my sister, but knew I could never live up to her expectations. I had no desire to be a Super-Christian. For years they wrote me heartfelt letters and prayed that I would submit my entire life to Jesus for his master plan. It broke them when I wrote that I lost my virginity. They felt pain that I had not waited for God's best for me. And then came the rehabilitation plans, as though I was a recovering addict.

Even my sister couldn't deny one thing, "I can see how that if you have made the decision not to be a Christian, you would feel so much more free."

That summer, my dad and I went on a lot of walks. He was trying to guide me back on the right path. "I came close to death before I was a Christian, and if I had died then, I would be in hell," he said.

I wondered if that was his only reason – fear. It seemed highly unlikely, that he would have become a Christian if it hadn't been for my mom. He had a choice – divorce or convert. Up to that point, I'm sure my mom drove him crazy with her zealousness. But once he joined the club, it didn't seem so bad. He finally became a member of our worship song singing family. And though I was happy as a child to have my father more involved, it was sad that he no longer did his own thing, or hung out with his buddies drinking beers. He stopped seeing his friend altogether. His sole purpose now was to look out for us and protect his brood from all things "of the world." But being protected prepares you for nothing.

On our walk he asked me, "Do you still feel that you are a Christian?"

"I don't know. I don't want to be a mediocre Christian. What's the point in that? If I'm going to be a Christian, it has to be the most passionate, whole-hearted thing of my life."

My dad waved his hand back and forth. "You don't have to be passionate. You just have to follow. God will take care of the rest."

Chapter 39

*"He who makes a beast of himself
gets rid of the pain of being a man."*

Samuel Johnson

Under the full moon, down the runway of the sidewalk, I paraded for a non-existent audience in a design of my own creation. Cut, pinned and sewn, diamond shapes of rust ultra suede created a mermaid silhouette, topped off with midriff-baring fringe. Pheasant feathers extended from my platinum hair, and peacock plumes fluttered from the stems in my clutching hand. I felt empowered and thought of my theme, the phoenix rising from the ashes.

As one foot half circled the other, my hips teeter-tottered. It seemed wrong to be arriving to a party in such an extravagant costume with no one to walk in with. The oncoming solitary entrance gave me anxiety.

I arrived to the pulsing, glowing house and felt queasy at the gate of Irving's yard. A dark stranger stood outside watching me and I greeted him as he regarded my ensemble.

"I made it myself!" I exclaimed, swooping my feathers

through the air.

"You're not serious! It's amazing. It's sexy! It's incredible. The party awaits you." He gestured his arm toward the door, and I ascended the stairs and entered.

Faint familiarities danced in corsets with wigs of rainbow thoughts. Vixens in black vied for adoration. Boas billowed and fake eyelashes blinked. The entire menagerie seemed to spin in a circle like painted horses on a carousel. But most shocking was the fact that Irving had shipped out all of his furniture for the night.

I was checked off the guest list. A glass broke, and Irving appeared. He seemed dazed by the grandness of his creation, surfacing here and there amidst small catastrophes. I tickled his neck with my feathers, he kissed me lightly, and I moved quickly on my way before we had to suffer through awkward conversation.

Through a gust of streamers, Nico burst through the door. He wore his black body-clutching tube dress. I felt both content and unnerved at the sight of him. We had argued over this party because he wanted to go alone. I understood, but felt wary of all the ways he could hurt me. We kissed and said hello, and then he sped off to partake of the experiences found in each different room.

Uncertain of what to do with myself, I proceeded to the dance floor, where I collided with Ilan, Irving's playboy twin from Florida. I hadn't known he was engaged when we first met at the Pajama Party. He invited me to dance and I smiled, happy at least to interact with someone who wouldn't dash away constantly.

"You know, I most prefer to either date an Aries or a Leo," I said, glancing back at Irving, "Pisces can be a little hard to reach, Cancers are too into house and home, and I tend to feel a disconnect with people born in the fall or winter," I said. "What sign is your fiancé?"

He looked at me, a little stunned. Then laughed, "Well, she's a Cancer."

"If you're going to settle down, that's a good way to go."

His shoulders slumped, and he looked deflated. We

danced into different directions and in a moment of eye contact the party began. The most beautiful stranger I had seen all night smiled at me from across the room. I glanced from side to side nervously. He walked over and smiled at me with a crooked grin. He was tall and striking, wearing a ridiculous pair of bat wings.

"Are you having fun?" he asked.

"I'm working on it. A bit more wine and I'll be there."

His blue eyes glinted in the flashing lights, making him appear mischievous.

"It's wonderful visiting all these beautiful people here in Seattle," he said, gesturing across the room with his red plastic cup.

"You're not from here?"

"I'm from the Bay area, but I'm trying to get into graduate school at the University of Washington."

"Wonderful!"

"Listen, you must try some absinthe. I discovered it upstairs," he said, in an aside.

"How bohemian. I'd love to."

"It's the real thing," he said, offering me some of his.

One tiny sip and waves of ecstasy rushed over my skin, seeping all through me. Feelings of love emanated through the room and I was suddenly intertwined with all of humankind, not on the outside looking in, but within all of it as one.

"It tastes like lavender," I said.

The stranger and I greedily shared it between us, saying, "One more sip, just one more." The plastic glass jumped back and forth between our clutching hands.

"Have you been to Burning Man yet?" he asked.

"No, not yet. Maybe I need to become more depraved first."

"And what is it you need to do that?"

"I need sin! Decadent sin! And corruption!" My arms flailed dramatically and I threw my head back.

He laughed over my absinthe-induced proclamations.

"It's a pain being so intelligent," I mused. "I can never

stop thinking so much. Sometimes I can't reach an orgasm because I'm thinking, thinking, thinking, analyzing every single little feeling till it kills every one."

"I know exactly what you mean! My mind is always in the way. It's so hard to relax when there are so many thoughts in your head."

"I wonder if there is more absinthe upstairs?"

"We should find out."

"You know, we really should," I agreed.

We ascended the stairs, the beautiful stranger supporting me as I tripped over my difficult costume. Turning the bend, the guest bedroom was laden with mattresses, red lights, and a man who served absinthe. I held out our glass, "We're in need of more."

The man, who was wearing a devil's costume, grinned, the neck of the bottle hanging from his hand, "Only if you give me a kiss. This stuff isn't given for free."

I kissed him and just like magic, my glass was half full. I gazed happily at the nasty brown liquid, and returned to my bat-winged fairy man leaning up against the wall levitating in a daze. Below us on the mattresses a couple slithered under the covers. I threw up my hand and cheered, "Copulate away! Copulate away!"

The fairy man emptied my mouth of words with a kiss. I was lost inside his lips, and time disappeared into giddy intoxication. An urge floated around my brain to tell him that I loved him, but before I could, absinthe spilled on my fringe and I needed to be steadied. He started to giggle. We stared at each other in a ridiculous manner and swooned. He seemed to be examining my face in an incredulous manner, but then felt jaded and mocked the experience with a laugh. We kissed again.

I was aware of another presence, and turned to face a girl in a pink wig. Then from the mattress, Nico's friend George called, "Why don't you both join us?" He wore a demented grin and was clutching at a woman I'd never seen before.

I turned back to the girl next to me, who blurred and kissed me passionately. I fell into that strange feeling of soft on soft. The bizarre pillows of her lips, her smiling face, pink hair disappearing into heavy air, bodies moving in an out of view, backwards and forwards.

"You know that's really not fair," stated the bat-winged fairy. "She didn't kiss me!"

"She doesn't want you! She just wants me!" I laughed as he kissed her. His friend materialized from the darkness, "Hey, we have to go now."

"But I'm busy, terribly busy."

"Five minutes then, unless you want to go home with her."

"I'm afraid that wouldn't work. What would my parents think, finding a bat-winged fairy in my bed?" I asked.

"Yes, that wouldn't work at all. I guess I have to go then."

"I guess you do."

We kissed and clung to each other. I didn't want him to leave. He was my one happy place. The place where I knew nothing could go wrong. He descended the stairs and I soon followed, not interested in hiding out with an overweight woman in the coatroom who wanted to share her woes. I stumbled onto the dessert table where Steffen, a portly Belgian billionaire, was indulging in the sweets.

"You must try the chocolate covered strawberries," he said, placing one in my mouth, and then another. I felt hypnotized by his sweaty face, painted designs streaking down with perspiration. His large eyes meandered blankly. Juices burst through chocolate onto my tongue. I swallowed slowly and watched him take the last bites for himself.

"I must get another drink," I stated.

"Then we shall get one for you. I will take you into the depths and it shall be beautiful," he said, with a dramatic flourish.

Descending to the basement, I helped myself to a drink, since the topless bartender girls were too busy dancing. Steffen led me away towards a curtained area in back.

"What is this little room here?" I asked.

"I don't know, we must find out." He pulled back the curtain and there stood a silver sparkling sex machine, resembling a dentist chair.

"My goodness!" I exclaimed.

"We must press the button."

The ridiculous contraption began to jiggle all over while the dildo went mad with the dead giveaway noise of a lawn mower engine.

"You must try this lovely thing out!"

"Oh no, oh no! You first!"

"No, no. I know what we must do. We must make love in this little sex machine room. It will be lovely!"

"No! I must escape from the clutches of Steffen!"

"Just one kiss."

And there I was, up against the sex machine, being kissed, with a large klutzy hand sneaking its way down my very tight skirt.

"I must escape!" I exclaimed, as I pushed him aside and performed a disappearing act through the curtain.

Upstairs in the kitchen I was drawn towards the beautiful breasts of a very young woman. How refreshing to find such comfort in two perfect round things. I caressed them and pondered how lovely it would be to fall in head first, right in between them, and bounce around micro-sized in the luminous flesh.

Another beautiful boy appeared. He was dressed in silk pajama pants and a rainbow vest, with ear length dreadlocks and compassionate eyes. He poured me a glass of water and surprised me with tales of his celibate life. "It's in my nature to be alone now, from waiting so long. I grew up in a conservative environment, where sex only belongs in marriage."

"What kind of conservative?"

"Christian."

"So did I!"

"Really?" His eyes lit up with recognition. We walked to the deck and looked down at all the people surrounding the bon fire.

"That's my lover down there," I said to the beautiful man, "the one who is kissing that girl." I wondered why I was

telling him this and ruining my chances. But then I
remembered he wouldn't sleep with me anyway.

"Ah yes, Nico."

From beside me a voice burst out, "What a divine
costume you're wearing!"

I turned to face an extravagant drag queen, dressed in a
black cowboy hat, a boa, and a tightly cinched corset.

"Oh thank you so much! I made it myself."

"Get out of town! You should design costumes for me!"

"Serious? I can't believe this turned out," I said, pinching
my tight skirt and running my fingers through the fringe.

All three of us paraded down to the lawn and Nico
swooped over to me, grasped me in his arms and kissed me.
"Would you like to come home with me?" he asked.

"Of course I would!"

"Oh good! You will be my ride, so please don't leave with
someone else. You won't leave with someone else, will you?"

"No, I won't."

"Did you meet Drew? The drag queen?"

"Yes, I did!"

"She is the highest paid drag queen in the entire
country!"

"Really! He, I mean she, is so fabulous! Drew we love
you!" Nico and I clung to each other as we rushed over to
Drew, each sucking a nipple of the towering drag queen with
the monstrous fake eyelashes.

"Oh! Such heaven! You two are too much!"

Nico turned to me, "Lauren, you are a fabulous drunk.
And your costume is perfect. Hold my cigarette!"

He handed it to me, and I took a drag, and then another
as smoke from the bonfire blew into my face. "Drew, you are
beautiful!" I called from several feet away.

I turned to the boy in dreadlocks and told him what a
perfect body he had, admiring with my hands, the fat-free
chest of him. "Everyone is just so fabulous!" I proclaimed, in a
drunken epiphany.

"Do you see that Swedish girl over there?" asked Nico,
pointing to a fairy-like creature covered in glitter with short

dark hair. "She's had sex with like six people at the party tonight. What a slut!"

I admired her beautiful charisma, like an otherworldly creature, and wished that I could be her. The chill in the air was too much and we all went back inside and proceeded to the dance floor. I danced with Nico's friend Leonardo, as Nico and Irving danced close by.

"I have been watching you all night," whispered Leonardo into my ear. "You make a beautiful blonde. I like your hair this way. You are sooo sexy."

I laughed. Peter appeared behind me, the English teacher I had met at Irving's birthday party. We danced and he gazed at me with a tormented expression typical of writers.

"Are you having a good time?" he asked.

"Oh, yes, I mean, it's all a little over-stimulating, but it's such an excellent party. I think Irving really topped himself on this one."

"Did you see that Swedish girl? The one that looks like an elf?"

"Yeah, I did," I replied.

"She's slept with like twelve people tonight. Isn't that crazy?" he asked.

"You know, back in the sixties when people were just learning about the magnitude of female sexuality, this woman wanted to set the record for how many men she could sleep with consecutively in one night. She slept with over ninety, and then when they interviewed her she said she still wanted more and wasn't completely satisfied."

"The fear and the fantasy of every man, right?"

"I think so! The insatiable female! I don't even think Nico could play that stunt."

Soon we went upstairs and there was Nico, stimulating a naked girl with his fingers. A group of onlookers leered down at her. Nico lurched on the floor with a grin on his face. The girl writhed and wriggled, loudly vocalizing a series of high-pitched ethereal moans. The sound struck a hateful tone in my ears. She repulsed me immensely, like the foul stench of a hog greedily snorting through slops. Her anemic little body lunged, pale and sickly under the red light. It felt as though someone had just thrust a dagger through my stomach. I hunched over, frozen.

All of my denial, and all of my fear swelled up in my throat. Every woman possessed the same replaceable anatomy. The interchangeability of sex made me feel as though I was nothing. No matter what I did, there was always another woman to replace me.

I turned to Peter, "I can't believe I saw that. I can't believe I saw that." Shaking, I rushed down the stairs trying to escape.

He followed behind, "You need air. Lets go outside."

We stood in the garden, and Peter gave me his heavy coat. My shoulders slumped under the weight.

"Are you okay?" he asked.

I stood there saying nothing, blankly staring at the stunted palm tree imprisoned in the corner of the white picket fence.

"I love this garden. You can tell a very eccentric person created it." I pretended that everything was normal, and smiled at Peter, feeling shy.

"You know, Irving and Nico are larger than life. They are amazing people. But you have to be careful."

"I know. I can't believe I saw that. I can deal with it, as long as I don't see it, you know? We all like to feel we are unique, right? That made me feel I am just one of the mass. And nothing I can give will ever really register with them."

"It's often extraordinary to hang out with those guys, but I love the peacefulness of my other friends too."

"It's nice to have a balance. I've only felt intense hatred for the people I've loved the most. Isn't that ironic? You have to be out of your mind with love, to ever be out of your mind with hate."

"I don't know about that," said Peter. He went silent for a moment, fiddling with his hat. "Lauren, kiss me."

I kissed him and smiled. There was always someone willing to save the damsel in distress and resolve it with that simple statement, 'Kiss me!' Every kiss of the night ran together into one, and I could no longer decipher what was left of reality. Was I even living in reality? It seemed more like someone else's fucked up fantasy.

"I have to leave now," said Peter, looking sheepishly up at me through his black- rimmed glasses.

"Okay. Let's stay in touch."

"You know, you can come home with me if you want. I'm staying three blocks from here. Are you sure you're okay?"

"Yes, I'm fine."

"Bye Lauren," he waved, walking down the sidewalk.

I stood there in my extravagant costume, plumes of peacock feathers in my hand. I went back in and the entire front room was empty. The music played from a machine. The blue and red lights were strange and harsh with no one beneath them. Downstairs the topless women flopped. Drew whispered to a boy in a swing until they were enveloped in a knot of arms. I searched for Nico because I wanted to leave, but I couldn't find him.

In Irving's bedroom, five or six naked people slithered in a knot on the bed. A dimpled white ass loomed in the air, and a wave of familiarity washed over me as I recognized it as Irving. I remembered being in this bedroom, with his candles and his music and my constant frustration at being refused by him when I had always wanted more. I missed his appreciation of my traits, and the ways in which I made him laugh. There were many ways in which I had felt more connected to Irving.

"Is Nico in here?"

"No, he's not," someone said in the darkness.

I went downstairs, "Has anyone seen Nico?"

"Isn't he upstairs? I hear him singing," a girl said.

From a distance I heard, "Strange, I've seen that face before!" He'd had that Grace Jones song stuck in his head for the past five months. Every bit of his personality steeped in my system. What a horrible singing voice. So horrible it was charming.

"No, he's in the basement." And was he? I gazed around, feeling out of sorts. Two men appeared and I held them, running my hands up their strong arms. Everything whirled together. "I want to go home, I want to go home."

And then he appeared, "Five more minutes!"

Exasperated I escaped to the backyard where the bonfire twirled, deserted and fading. I stared into it for a long time and thought about throwing my feather plumes into the fire, so the Phoenix could rise out of the ashes. I wanted to start something new, a baptism or cathartic experience, and really, my cats would destroy the feathers anyway. A black shadow flitted through the fence. "Francesco! I love you! I've missed you! Don't run away from me. Remember me!"

But the cat was more concerned with remaining a phantom in lieu of Irving's oblivion. I sat and let the smoke seep into the fabric embracing me tightly. I was happiest being alone. No one could hurt me within solitude. It was all so much effort. I strove to be the most attractive, the most interesting. But there was always another woman. And almost always they were much less attractive than I was. It wasn't about how they looked. It was about how much of a nymphomaniac they were. They appeared with all their mysteries to be solved, while I was adding bricks to my wall. My presence was growing stale, and I felt myself growing old. It was 6am. My thoughts were muddled and vague.

"I should leave without Nico," I said out loud. "I should leave. Why don't I leave? Why can't I? I can't. But I should."

I wandered back in and sat on a couch. A man began rubbing my shoulders, "We're leaving now, are you going to be okay?"

"Yes, I'm fine. Sober. I think. I feel strange."

And then my emotions disintegrated. I stood up, anger coursing all through me. I clenched my fists, faced the stairs and yelled at the top of my lungs, "*Nico!* Get the *fuck* down here! I'm leaving! *Now!*"

I stormed to the front door, and Nico, in a state of shock, ran down the stairs throwing on his coat. I didn't wait for him. I kept on walking, bursting through the gauzy curtains at the entrance. My knees rubbed together under the skirt, my legs raced, curling around the other, slinking in fast-forward. Nico flew out onto the sidewalk, flailing and wild-eyed like a little boy who has been hurt immensely.

"*Wait* for me! Lauren! *Wait!*" He caught up with me and followed behind as I raced down the street.

"I *hate* you! You don't *care* about me! I'm not having sex with you tonight! I can't, I can't!" I reasoned, flailing my hands as though I was throwing garbage on the ground.

"Oh! That's just fine. Do whatever you want!"

"I saw you giving that girl an orgasm. It was disgusting. You've gotten enough for one night!"

"What was disgusting about it? It was beautiful! I had sex with eight people, and I never used my penis. It was so beautiful."

We sped down the street, fuming.

"How can you say I don't *care* about you?" he asked. "You wouldn't be *here* with me! Coming *home* with me! If I didn't care about you! I don't even know those people! I was just giving them pleasure. Tell me! What was disgusting?"

"It hurt me. It hurts."

"Is it disgusting when I sleep with you?"

"No, it isn't. It isn't. It's beautiful. In the moment in there, it was so disgusting. I'm not jealous, I'm hurt."

"Lauren, Lauren," he pleaded, taking me by the shoulders.

I looked down at the sidewalk. Tears fell across my face.

"Lauren, look at me."

I looked at him with my head cocked, half facing him, half not.

"Lauren, we are friends. Lauren, I love you," he said, holding me. "You can say it back, I know you love me."

I felt too vulnerable to let the words run free. "I love you," I answered finally, in defeat. My face was buried in his neck.

"Someday you will be happy for me. You will be happy for my freedom."

"Maybe."

He let go of me, and we got into my car. He turned off the stereo and spoke a trail of words that didn't make any sense. His banter melted my anger. I felt pathetic and too aroused to be strong.

We arrived to his house and he asked me to help take off his boots. I knelt down on the kitchen floor and held his leg, pressing my cheek against the inside of his knee as I undid the buckle and zipper. I pulled and yanked on the clunky black boot and we laughed as I took off the other. He heated a bowl of minestrone for me and made scrambled eggs for himself. Nico turned to me, "We need to just love each other."

I was seated at the kitchen table and he stood above me. I wrapped my arms around his waist, and pressed my head against his abdomen, savoring each curve and comfort of his being. He sat, and while we ate, our eyes connected over the table, and we smiled anxiously at each other. I felt so angry for wanting him.

"Lauren. You are in charge. You are in control. Everything is the way you see it now. But you can change the way you see."

"What do you mean?"

"You are the victim. But someday you will be above that."

I looked at him feeling confused. My head felt like an unbearable weight on my shoulders and my vision was blocked from seeing beyond the pain I felt.

We finished and went downstairs. I laid on the bed and looked into his eyes, but he wasn't there. He was moving through motions, but the blankness was like making love to a corpse. Death seeped into my body. I felt nothing but fear as he turned me over. He railed with all his strength, splitting through my rectum. My scream ripped through the silent house. I dug all ten fingers hard into the edge of the mattress. The air in the room felt freezing cold.

I sobbed over the side of the bed, and he took my limp body into his arms.

"Oh baby, be quiet. What have I done to you? Shhh. It's okay," he rocked me back and forth like a child, "It's okay. I'll never do it again. I promise. I never meant to hurt you. Shhh. Be quiet now."

My tears subsided and his fingers caressed my wet face. He brushed my hair back from my forehead and kissed me gently.

"See? You're okay now. You're okay." He rocked me and his fingers wandered down between my thighs. "There, there," he said, cooing like a mother. He placed me on his hips and gently began thrusting slowly, in and out.

"Are you here Nico? Where are you?"

"I'm right here. I'll always be here."

"I do love you."

"Of course you do."

I gazed into his face, but his eyes were blank and glazed over with dank alleyways and long ago nights suppressed somewhere in his subconscious. It seemed he was looking through me to the wall. I questioned why I was there. But then the rhythms were overtaking me again. Starving for him I felt the pangs of a wild animal, my hips circling across his thighs. He grasped my weight and threw me stomach down on the bed, once again slamming into my ass as blood came down.

Chapter 40

When I woke up I turned to find myself alone. I heard Nico rustling upstairs in the kitchen. My head was pounding as I crawled into my clothes and shuffled up the stairs in a lethargic haze.

"Morning," I said, passing Nico in the kitchen and heading straight for the couch to curl up in a corner.

"It's a beautiful day Lauren!"

"Is it?"

"I have so much to do today. I have to leave soon, but I'll make you toast."

I rubbed my sleepy eyes with my fists as my golden hair flopped over my forehead.

"What a party!" he exclaimed. "Did we sleep together last night? I can't even remember!"

"Ugh. Yeah. You don't remember at all?"

"I can barely remember leaving the party."

"That's convenient," I muttered quietly.

"What was that?"

I warred back and forth as to whether I should say anything or pretend certain things never happened, never existed, never were incurred on me. It would cause him pain to know the truth if he really did not remember. Otherwise the claim of a blackout was a convenient cover for his actions. But he *had* blacked out. I'd seen it in his face. I'd been afraid because I knew he wasn't there. All that he hadn't forgiven in his life lived on in his subconscious, and I had been in the way.

"Oh nothing," I replied. Burying it all down within me, I thrust my shoulders back, looking up at the ceiling to rise above my emotions. My lungs felt empty of air. I took in a deep breath.

It was different now, I knew. As my attachment to Nico grew, it was inevitable that he would pull away. I saw that the weave was slipping and soon I would fall backwards, back where I came from in boredom, routine, and loneliness. A sense of panic overcame me and I started to knead my loose t-shirt. I was losing him.

. . .

I sat across from Kristen and Ruth, two friends I kept in contact with from high school. I hadn't seen them in a while, and felt obliged to have brunch with them. Ruth wore an out-dated Hawaiian print button-up shirt with elastic band shorts. Her hair hung scraggly and shapeless, white legs poking out from under the table. It was as though it had never occurred to her to attract a man. Kristen wore khaki's with pleats in the front and a faded navy blue polo top. Her hair was pulled back in a tight ponytail with a thick layer of frizzy bangs shadowing the top of her face. There was an awkward silence between us as we ate our first bites. I wore all black with combat boots beneath my floor length skirt.

I wondered why I ever saw old friends. We no longer had anything in common except for the past. Even our memories of high school made it seem as though we had been in two different places. They had been top of the class, while I had been in the 'stupid people classes' as I liked to call them.

"So are you seeing anyone?" I asked Kristen.

"Oh no, not really," Kristen looked out the window. "Well, I kind of think this one guy from church is attractive. But I don't know. I would never just say anything. He seems very respectful and nice. I wouldn't really want to go out on a date. I'd just like to get to know him better."

"Well isn't that what a date is for?"

"I, um, I wouldn't want to imply that sort of interest."

"Hmm."

"Anyway, you know, I'm busy. I don't have time for those things."

"Well, when will you?"

"God's timing is always right."

"Sure, but didn't God give you this time of being single to be carefree for a little while?"

"I don't think so, Lauren," she grimaced. "How about you?"

"I'm not exclusive with anyone. But I've been hanging out with this Italian guy, Nico. We have a lot of fun together. He's absolutely crazy. It's inspiring. He helps me to leave my inhibitions behind."

"I'm sure he does," said Ruth.

"Are you sure you can trust him?" asked Kristen.

"He's very honest."

"That's not what I mean. I worry about you. I don't like to see you get hurt," said Kristen.

"I'm not hurting. I've been having the time of my life. And of course, I know how it will end. It's inevitable, but so what. I'm a strong person, and I know he'll always be my friend."

"But how many break-ups can you go through Lauren? Just don't do anything you will regret. There is some guy out there who is going to love you, respect you, value you, complete you, serve you, provide for you. You shouldn't settle for less. I know you have been physically involved with guys and it breaks my heart. I hate that you are letting yourself be used," said Ruth.

Kristen turned to me, "You should guard yourself

Lauren. It's not right."

"Well, I really don't see it that way. What's not right is being afraid of the world. I know that our choices are very different. But I'm happier than I've ever been. I was so depressed before. I couldn't express myself, no one understood me. A creative person needs to be free to grow, not restricted by rules and boundaries. I feel strong now. All I wanted before was to end my life, because I thought it would never begin."

"You've always been so dramatic."

I raised my eyebrows. "Yes, I know," I said, taking a sip of coffee. "Rules are meant to be broken. I got to the point in college where it seemed like the only purpose of having so many rules was to break them all, like rites of passage. The only rule I didn't break was the homosexual thing. My room-mate took care of that one."

"Why does everything have to be about rebelling?" Kristen asked, looking distressed.

"Well I wouldn't say it was about rebelling. It was about protesting our lack of rights as adults. Students might be kids when they get there, but they're adults when they leave."

"But being an adult doesn't mean you have to do stupid things like smoking and drinking. It means you take on responsibilities."

"Since when. The only responsibility I want, and not even want, is to pay my rent on time. I don't even get to do *that* right now. Beyond just being on my own I couldn't care less. Life is too short to buy into what everyone else tells you to do."

"I just want simplicity," spoke Kristen.

Ruth looked at me sideways and then took a long sip of coffee. "Well Lauren, you've changed. You change to be more like every man you see."

"What is that supposed to mean?"

Chapter 41

Nico was my only way of connecting to the self I wanted to become. Self-hatred crept up on me as I realized my own inability to be as fearless as he was, jealous of his freedom, his way of being. He was the master of his own reality, while I felt like a peon every single day of my life.

Where I came from, no one could understand why anyone would want to follow a path that led away from marriage, family, routine, corporations, houses, church on Sunday. Nico was my key to break beyond the trap door. I couldn't understand, why he even wanted me to be a part of his life. The thought of it helped me to begin loving myself. I was learning how to become who I knew I was all along. No longer did I stuff the truth down below. Words began to flow from me, more freely then they ever had before.

Being young, the freedom to make my own choices was a new concept. But I knew there must be a way to make my artistic ideas a reality. The sound of fluid words rolling off the tongue, vibrant colors like waterfalls, movements shooting through limbs like rays of light, a melody piercing the night with electricity palpable in the air. I wanted to create art from the beauty all around me. Maybe all the pain would show me how.

The dusk was dank and the air hung heavy, the sort of air that makes you notice the trash on the street lining gutters from long gone nights. Left to disintegrate, it had decomposed into smaller and smaller particles, colors erased to bits of dead dirty whiteness.

Nico, his friend George, and I walked down Pike Street from a sex shop where George had purchased a cock ring so that he could last longer. It was the first time I had seen such a large display of sex toys. I marveled over all the colorful dildos, strange bondage contraptions, and flavored lubes. We had only walked two blocks away when a crazed looking homeless man appeared in front of us. None of us were certain where he had come from. He stood in our path with his hair hanging down around his beard, above tattered layers of misshapen clothing.

"What's a girl like *you* doing walking down the street with *fags*? What are they going to do for you? Huh? Nothin'! *Fuckin'* fags. I could screw you better than they *ever* could."

"*Fuck* off, man," spat Nico, as we passed. The man acted as though he would follow us to keep taunting, but lost the nerve. We walked away quietly feeling upset, our day violated by someone else's hate.

Later that night at the Catwalk Nightclub, I spent most of my time dancing alone while admiring an exotic woman in full corset with bloomers and a fan. She danced with command, flipping the fan against her wealthy bosom that shook with the pulsing rhythm. This woman must have been forty, and I envied her assurance. She did not need anyone's identity to define her own, and the room spun around her axis.

Watching her, I doubted myself even more. Would I ever be free of obsessive love, able to stand on my own without thoughts consistently circling around some man with a wandering attention span? I roamed the black sticky floors in search of confidence. But instead I found Nico in the back, his lips locked with those of a tall redhead. I stood in front of them for a few moments. The woman noticed me and pulled away, her red lips twisted by a smirk. I glared. The woman took in my youth and I felt insignificant, once again.

"Lauren."

"Yes."

"This is my friend Delta. She's a Dominatrix."

"Wonderful," I said, without putting out my hand. "I'm tired. Definitely ready to go home." If there was one thing I could exert over other women, it was the ability to say I was going home with the man they were kissing.

"Have a lovely night, Nico," Delta said, running her index finger down the curve of his chin and turning to walk away.

"What was *that?*" I asked.

Nico pretended he hadn't heard. "Lets go," he said, taking my hand and leading me away.

"Sometimes I just wish we could always be alone. You drive me crazy."

"You know you can't change me."

"I never said I would try."

In the car he began to stroke my thigh. I felt intoxicated and luminous under his touch. His hand moved upwards as he drove down empty late night streets, past empty warehouses, in the rain. His fingers reached to unzip my vinyl hot pants. Quickly he smoothed his hand down the front.

I maneuvered onto my stomach with the chair back, shorts down around my ankles, waving my ass in the air as his fingers dove in and out. Industrial music blared through the car with the usual sound effects of whips and lashes and a thumping bass beat. The stench from the mulled wine that had tipped on the way to the nightclub was nauseating. He had made 5 gallons for the event that night.

At the house, I ran downstairs and stripped off all my clothes, putting on Nico's black underwear instead. I ran up to where he stood making eggs and stuffed an apple down the front of the briefs. I went charging through the living room, flailing my long limbs like a marionette, "Look, I'm a man, I'm a man, I'm a man!"

"Ha-ha!"

"What do you think about my big dick?" I called, patting my apple bulge.

"It looks delicious and sweet."

"Yeah. Take a bite out of that one will you!" I collapsed on the floor laughing hysterically.

He sat on the chair laughing with me, looking down.

"Why do you have to drive me crazy?" I asked.

"Because, you wouldn't care about me if I didn't," he said. He bent down to kiss my neck and we fell into each other unable to stop when it should have been over.

Chapter 42

In April 2001 I graduated from college feeling much more like a writer than the future fashion designer I had planned on being. I was writing every single day, while my technical skills as a designer had failed me. I didn't care if I never saw another sewing machine again. Adding to my angst, a guy that I liked had seen me in the sewing lab and said to me, "It's so good to see that you're learning how to be a happy housewife!" I hope he was being sarcastic. But for most of the other girls in my program, it could have been the truth.

In June, I moved into an early twentieth century studio apartment on 21st and Glisan Street in Portland. It had an icebox, hardwood parquet floors, and high ceilings. I lined the woodwork above my doors with glamorous collages of the Gabor sisters mixed with cutouts of precious gems. Outside my window, there was a terrific view of a ridiculously handsome gay guy who hosed the sidewalk enticingly in front of his flower stand next to Trader Joe's.

It wasn't long before I went crazy living alone in a shoebox. I needed instant love, so I went to the Animal Shelter. The older cat I had come to see didn't want to have anything to do with me. A Siamese kitten named Schrodinger was already on a waiting list. The girl who was working with me, a punk lesbian from the East Side, told me, "I think I know what might be right for you, but there are two of them."

She came back with two Burmese kittens, identical brothers. She set them down and immediately they jumped to either side of me and began licking my fingers in unison.

"Oh, I'm in love."

"Where do you live?" she asked.

"Northwest Portland."

"I see it now!" she exclaimed. "You're wearing a long black evening dress and they're on either side of you."

"Oh my gosh! I see it too! I'll take them!"

Sales tactics aside, I knew they needed to be together for life. They complemented each other. The next day, when they were ready, I took them home and named them Gucci and Valentino. They had a bad case of kennel cough and were sneezing snot everywhere. They jumped all over the bed for twenty minutes straight after I turned the lights out. Night owls, just like me. They tore down the curtains, knocked over the lamp, and dumped out garbage in the kitchen. Valentino liked to eat toilet paper. He would come charging out of the bathroom with it in his mouth to see how far he could get.

In the mornings, I couldn't help but forgive them. They snuggled up on my pillow and licked my ears and nose, tickling me until I woke up. It was impossible to stay in a funk with them around. They always made me laugh.

I had the apartment and the perfect pair of cats. There were plenty of coffee shops where I could write, and the New York Pizza place was just a few blocks away. The only thing missing was a job. No one would hire me. They all said, "Come back in September." I kept running out of money, getting down to pennies because I was too embarrassed to call home and ask for more. With no money and no employment I was bored and lonely. You can only read and write and wander for so long.

It seemed like the few straight men in my neighborhood (a rarity) were all determined to hit on me. I was careless

enough to actually have coffee with a guy who followed me for
blocks. I didn't know how to make friends in the assertive
role. I just let life happen to me. And people came. Nomads
and eccentrics, and ne'er do wells.

In college our professors had promised us that in our first
year out of school we would all be making $30,000 a year. I
have yet to make that much. Half of my classmates ended up
working at Starbucks. I finally got hired working two retail
jobs, and a few weeks later 9/11 hit. The day after that, I was
let go from *both* jobs. I was the expendable new hire. I felt
guilty that my parents were supporting me and the tension
grew.

I walked around everyday in a lethargic haze - drifting,
trying not to spend money, starving for sex. I slept with a lot
of people that I didn't really want to, just for the adrenaline
fix. My friends were disappointed with me for making bad
choices. But I felt like an addict. I needed to be wanted. I
needed the rush. I wanted to lose myself.

In September, I finally met a man I could adore. Carter.
We wrote each other intense, passionate, poem-riddled letters
and on our first date he brought me freesias and a book by
Nicholson Baker. He was handsome and tall with the look of
Clark Kent. We were giddy over each other. We had a knack
for being the first people at the restaurant, and the last to
leave. We could talk on the phone for eight hours straight and
wonder where the time went. He liked to hole up in my
apartment with me and watch old movies. He left things
behind, as security that he would be back.

But Carter wasn't exactly the ideal man. He had plans
for the perfect fail-proof suicide. It didn't help that he lived
alone in his dead grandmother's house and had phases of
extreme reclusion. He spent hours arranging things, seeking
perfection.

Carter had been a performance artist, and at one point
had buried himself alive. For another project he enlarged
1950's yearbook photos and hung plaster masks in front of
them on the wall. He labeled the masks with all the different
things he had done to them to reach into the past – kissed,

licked, pinched, touched.

One day, after a series of intense weekends together, he flipped out on me. He joined the Army Reserves and shaved his head. He couldn't love me enough, he said. So he had to leave. He went from being clean-shaven with well-tailored shirts to being a grungy guy in vintage. Then he wondered if they would let him bring his silk throw pillows to the base. I was confused. He told me never to contact him again. For good measure, he changed his phone number and email address. He disappeared completely.

Everywhere I went without him, the city seemed empty. I walked through blocks of deserted warehouses to Powell's bookstore, and drifted from aisle to aisle for hours. I went salsa dancing with my partner Rodolfo. He showed me the house he was building in Mexico City, and I got the feeling he hoped I would join him there.

Men all began to seem like predators, either trying to take away my freedom, or just trying to get me to sleep with them. I was exactly what they were all looking for – young, naïve, weak, open to anything.

I had briefly dated a man twenty years older in the last year of college. We stayed friends and wrote to each other constantly. He berated me for not being strong enough with men, then dropped hints that we should hook up with no strings attached. At the last minute he always found an excuse not to meet up. All of my new guy friends, too, seemed to be waiting for a weak moment.

The letters from my sister and brother in-law grew more and more intense. My brother in-law compared me to a tree that was sprouting rotting fruit. He told me I was making my parents feel like failures. My sister was determined to get me to rehabilitate and break the soul ties that were connecting me to the people I had slept with in the past. And always, always, "We don't condemn you. God can make you new again."

All I wanted, when I read these words, was to please them. I looked up to them and worshipped the love they gave to me. But their requests were not in my nature. I didn't want to move home, but I felt that my sister and brother in-law were right. Maybe I just needed to be in a safe place where I could learn how to be a Christian again. The Bible promised I could be made new in Christ. Everyone in my family and the subculture I was raised in believed this, so it must be true. But had it ever worked for me?

My brother in-law promised that God could restore me and make me like new. But I still don't understand the value of innocence. Innocence is for children, and I am an adult. As an adult I see no value in safety, protection, naïveté. Why would I want to return to the prison from which I escaped?

When I moved home that winter, my life took a turn in a different direction, and my family began to realize I wasn't going to change.

Chapter 43

"It seems obvious, doesn't it, that someone
who is ignored and overlooked
will expand to the point where they have to be noticed,
even if the noticing is fear and disgust."

Jeanette Winterson

Irving was throwing a party to glorify the one he'd
already had. A friend with a loft on Capitol Hill had offered to
host. It was a beautiful space with cherry wood throughout,
and a modern interior. Located right in the heart of the
neighborhood.

Initially, when I arrived at a party, I never knew what to
do with my hands. They felt unbearably empty, an emptiness
that I longed to fill with a glass of liquor or the swooping
gestures of conversation. Anything to get past the anxiety of a
room full of people I didn't know. I downed my first drink in
great gulps as though I was consuming eternal life.

I had arrived appropriately dressed to go to the Vogue
nightclub afterwards, which was just down the street. Irving
surveyed my five-inch platform shoes and fishnets clinging all

the way up to my vinyl-clad ass. He seemed unable to fully recognize me. I was coming down the stairs, when he approached looking hesitant.

"Hello," I said.

"How are you?" he asked.

"I'm good, how are you?"

"I'm fine."

"That's good," I replied. I towered over him for six seconds of silence. It was obvious then, that there was nothing left. I smiled uncomfortably, stepping down the last stair to walk away.

Against the kitchen counter there was a tall man with curly chestnut hair, light blue eyes and glowing skin. I'd never seen him before, and my attire magnetized him. "Wow," was all he could say three times over as I spun around for him. I noticed Irving still watching me, but I was staring at the door where Nico had just exited with another woman. She had arrived with the tall man. I knew Nico was probably just outside smoking, but I imagined his hands all over the beautiful woman on the stairs. What if they had just left together?

"So I did Ecstasy at this party last week," said the tall man, "and I felt like a kid again. You know, I'm older now and I wasted a lot of time when I was younger. These days I just focus on growing my business. But last week, wow. No inhibitions, you know?"

"I don't really do that stuff, but I can imagine. Sometimes I think I'm tripping just from dancing all night. I look around and realize I'm the only person not on something."

"Well, you should try it sometime."

"I'm not really interested. I read that if you take too much, in five years you could have signs akin to Alzheimer's. I depend on my memory too much for that. I hate forgetting things."

"Ha! Well, maybe you're smarter than the rest of us," he joked. "I know I've said it already, but I just love your fishnets," he said, looking down. "I can't stop looking at your ass."

I laughed nervously, sipping my drink at quickening paces.

He looked up towards the bedroom. "Maybe we should take a tour of the loft upstairs. This place is awesome. I love all the wood and the high ceilings. I'm an Architect actually," he said.

"Ooh, fantastic," I replied. He led me up, and I admired the way he looked, like he'd gone to an Ivy League school or posed for a Ralph Lauren ad. He could have been broke, but he had the aura of richness. Visions of yachts and polo and hunter green walls with built in mahogany bookcases filled my head.

Upstairs it was obvious his only motive was to have me pinned down on the chaise longue. He kissed me and for once it felt good to be in another man's arms. Though his desire was strong, there was a simplicity that didn't feel threatening at all. Would all men feel so basic after Nico?

We looked down from the railing as a projector was set up to screen a film of Irving's wild party. James had shot and edited the feature, and as we watched, it was obvious what turned him on the most – an over-abundance of girl on girl footage. The film ended with a slideshow and a voiceover of me reading a poem I had written about the event. I liked hearing my voice. It was not the uncertain, wavering nasal sound of just a few years ago. It sounded strong, sexy, and peaceful; my poem, a perverse bedtime story.

A few people congratulated me, but most didn't know that it was my voice or poem on the film. We all gathered up our coats, and made our way down the street towards the Vogue.

Once there, I somehow attracted an entourage of adoring men - Franco the aging millionaire, a man in a leather coat and dark sunglasses, and Ivy League (though it was obvious this wasn't his scene). I was blind to all of them. The liquor had crawled on top of me; it sloshed around in my brain, causing me to feel exuberant in one instant and desperate in the next. Nico appeared from the back room of ill adventures. He was approaching quickly and all I wanted was to be alone with him. I tripped over my heels and threw my arms around him as everyone looked on.

"Take me home with you. Why won't you?" I begged.

"I promised myself I wouldn't go home with anyone tonight."

"You don't care about me."

"I am trying to care about myself," he said flatly.

"What else is new," I mumbled.

Franco appeared with another Long Island. I couldn't even walk at this point, and needed to be guided around like an invalid. Any of the men would gladly have taken me home, yet I had to be obsessed with the one who wouldn't. Irving was still watching me, but his expression told me how foolish I looked. He danced with a stout woman who had black eyes and skin an afterlife white. He turned his back on me with a grimace.

. . .

"I'm going to be sick," I moaned, "I've never felt like this before."

Ivy League pulled into a gas station. I couldn't remember his name or even if he'd ever told me what it was. "I'll buy some water," he said, exiting the car.

I desperately needed air so I opened the door. I looked down at my ridiculously tall stripper shoes. My feet felt strangled in them, and my toes were red where the peep-toe was cutting into my skin. I took them off and kicked them to the side. The windshield was spinning, and the gas station was a blur. The lights made me feel ill. Leaning onto the door, and holding my head above the pavement, I vomited. I threw up until there was nothing left and then started to dry heave.

"Oh my," said Ivy League as he neared the car. He walked around and got in, handing me some napkins. "Drink this," he said, handing me a bottle of water.

I drank and laid my head back. "I feel like dead weight."

He drove through Capitol Hill and parked. "We're here! I live on Vashon, but I'm house-sitting for a friend."

We walked up the stairs. Inside he helped me into a t-shirt, and then laid back on the futon in the living room.

"I'm really embarrassed. I swear I've never been that drunk before."

"It's no problem."

"I don't know what's wrong with me. I'm really losing it."

He looked into my eyes, which must have been a mess of smeared make-up. I contemplated his angular perfection. He was too beautiful for me. Just then, he lifted his head from the pillow and kissed me gently. I leaned into him and we clung to each other. I wondered how he could still want me. He must have been desperate, holed up on the island for too long. I held him tight as he maneuvered over me. Our clothes came off, and he was inside of me. Within twenty seconds he came. Disappointed, he rolled over and away from me. I was used to a marathon runner, not a twenty-second sprinter.

"I can do better," he said with determination. He made it to sixty seconds. For the third round, it was three minutes. I still felt disappointed, but impressed that he could get it up three times in a row. I was relieved to be with someone who seemed to have some sort of a soul with vulnerabilities. I shyly kissed him on the cheek and gazed at his clean-cut profile. His skin was silvery like the moon. He smiled at me as I drifted off.

The next morning he sat on the couch watching *The Price is Right*. "This stuff is so fucking funny," he laughed.

I gazed around the white room, confused by my surroundings. I had finally slept with someone else as Nico wished. It was a strange feeling, overlapped by a sense of empowerment. And then here was this beautiful man who I had found intimidating, and he was laughing over a stupid game show. He no longer seemed perfect. In fact, he was thoroughly out of touch.

I rushed to retrieve the extra clothes in my bag, and locked myself in the bathroom. Coming out, I called, "I can walk back."

"Are you sure?"

"It's no problem."

"Well, here's my business card. Call me."

"I will," I said, taking it and closing the front door behind me.

I lazily made my way back to the car with the giant shoes and tiny vinyl pieces stuffed in my bag. In my daytime clothes, Ivy League probably realized I was not the sex vixen of the night before. Sitting in the driver's seat, I looked down at my turtleneck sweater and jeans. Then I gazed into the rearview mirror where my face looked washed out and pale, stripped of all the make-up. I had fooled Ivy League with magic, and he had fooled me too. I phoned Nico.

"Baby!"

"Hi Nico. How are you?"

"Oh, I feel fine. But how are *you*?"

"I'm okay. Listen, I went home with that guy last night. I finally did it Nico, I slept with someone else, and it felt so strange."

"I'm so happy for you!"

"It wasn't all that great, but it felt kind of freeing at the same time. I think I understand how you want me to be now."

"Yes, I want you to be independent. You don't need to depend on anyone. You can just be free, the way I am."

"I'm learning, I guess."

"Of course you are. You just need to let go of being attached."

Chapter 44

Four months later, I was still living with my parents. My mother and I had a tradition of going to our favorite Italian restaurant when my dad was away on business. Though I was no longer in contact with Irving or Nico, our mutual passion for all things Italian lived on. We went to language lessons together on Tuesday and Thursday nights, and she enjoyed correcting my pronunciations.

"I feel very old since Nico," I confided, "As though I've lived through many loves, and many experiences, and will never find anything that will make me feel so alive again. Other men don't really compare."

"Well, that will pass with time. You'll get over it."

I had loved Nico, but he never fed my soul, only my body. Eventually, I stopped listening to anything he said. His words were all meaningless. A broken record of maxims, meant to shock and awe his rotating audience. He never listened, only waited for the moment when he could speak.

When he stopped answering my phone calls, I quickly understood. I had watched him shut down as my feelings grew, and it was inevitable. It always happened this way.

"I suppose if all I'm feeling is old, I've fared well compared to the other women," I said to my mom. I was always more open with her after enough time had passed. It felt so intimate, eating alone with her in the dimly lit setting.

"You're lucky. I mean, at least you don't have herpes or anything."

A current of shock passed through me. Did she know? Had she guessed it? As she spoke my secret, I knew this was my chance to finally be free.

"What? I mean, actually, I do."

"What do you mean?"

"I have herpes."

"Oh. You know, I wondered about that."

"Yeah, I got it over the holidays, when I had that UTI. It was my own fault. I don't hold it against him. He was honest."

"It's terrible that you've had to go through that. I'm so sorry."

"Oh, it's alright," I smiled, feeling shaky, "I'm learning how to deal with it. It's expensive, but there are natural remedies that I'm learning about."

My body had let me down, and I was in fear of it. Afraid every time my immune system was down, because then it would hit. It was always there, under my skin, festering, as though it was some alien entity residing at the base of my spine.

"I hardly know what to say, or what it is even," my mother's brow wrinkled in confusion. This was all so far from the realm of her experience.

"You probably think I got what I deserved."

"No, I don't. We are all susceptible to disease."

"Thanks, mom," I took her hand in mine and we looked out the window as I felt unvoiced questions wavering on her tongue.

"Pastor Dave said that you lose a part of yourself in every person that you sleep with," she said.

"I don't really think so. I feel like you *gain* something from every person. You find a new part of yourself. Every man I've ever loved has enriched me in some way. I think it is always really worth it, to love."

After the time in college when my father tried to kick me out of the house, he realized he didn't want to lose me. It took time, but with time came acceptance. He tried his best to never say a word of judgment, and I thought of it as part of his Christian journey. It's a difficult thing for a parent to accept when their child doesn't turn out according to the master plan. One side of me always tried so hard to be someone I was not, and the other side knew that none of it felt real. And then somehow the whole thing hinged on my sexuality. Sex was the beginning of my journey. It was how I learned to finally tell the truth. It was the end of living two parallel lives.

For a time after Nico, I found that I was no longer fantasizing about men. I began to sexually long for my own self. Longing to reclaim my body in a relinquishment of the control I had lost. And soon I quenched this feeling through wanting other women. My thoughts lingered on the softness of their skin, the gentleness of their intimacy. Swimming in their salty taste, lost in layers of emotion. At night I dreamt of the womb wide open to my thirst. Skin cleaving to skin, feathery touch, and the cushiony softness of a woman's lips.

With Nico I had been jealous of the other women. I no longer wanted to compete with them. He created these games to feel wanted, and I was no longer a player. Still, it lingered in my consciousness for years. I couldn't let go of it, though the game was lame and transparent. No one else could play it quite so well, with so many rotating players. Though I dated other men, there was nothing but the past.

When I finally saved enough money, moving to Seattle wasn't quite enough. There were too many things I wanted to run away from, too many memories. So I left it all behind and moved to New York. Three years of crazy times and struggles and constant movement went by and I was out of breath. I learned how to live my life without anyone else's influence. It seemed that anything was possible. Then Nico reappeared.

Chapter 45

While visiting my family for a week, I went to a party at Nico's house. In the kitchen, a guy named Pax smiled at me, blue eyes shining behind fragile spectacles. He had the delicate demeanor of an invalid with skin eggshell-white, blue veins crisscrossing along his hair-less arms. His nostrils flared softly above luscious lips that revealed prominent canines in a row of slightly crooked teeth.

"Why aren't you drinking?" I asked.

"I don't really drink, I don't like the way it makes me feel," said Pax.

"I don't smoke out for the same reason," I said, tossing the rest of my wine back and pouring some more.

"Are you okay?" he asked.

"Oh yeah. I guess there is just a lot of overwhelming energy in the room," I said, waving my hand back and forth.

"I specialize in energy. I am a healer. Here's my card," he said, flipping a rainbow-striped card from a metal clip, and handing it to me. It read, 'Healing & Massage.'

"I've never had a professional massage before."

"You should call me then. You carry a lot of tension in

your shoulders. I can help straighten that out."

"Yeah, I guess I *am* a little tense."

Looking down at the spread of food on the table, Pax hinted, "So, no one here is allowed to feed themselves?"

"Would you like a cucumber cream puff?" I asked.

"Definitely."

I gingerly lifted one from the platter and turned to place it in Pax's waiting mouth. He lingered over the flavors.

"Do you know Nico?" asked Pax.

"Oh yes, we dated a long time ago. We're still friends. Doesn't he throw the greatest parties?"

"He's something of a legend. I've heard so much about him, but we've never met. He really gets around."

"Yeah, I'm sure you'll meet him tonight." I assured him.

"Your dress is stunning by the way. It really accentuates your hips."

"Thank you," I said, as I looked down and pinched the fabric that clung to my waist. "Who did *you* come with tonight?" I asked.

"That group of people over there," he said pointing.

"I actually don't live in Seattle anymore," I confessed.

"Oh?"

"I've been living in New York for three years, but I miss it here. I miss the energy of people just being. In New York you always have to watch your back. Everyone is so busy trying to become something." I took a sip of my drink and gazed at Pax's ghost-like face over the rim of my cup. "You're a strange person. But I like strange. Everything else bores me," I said.

"Well, you should check out the chill space downstairs. Cushions everywhere and red lights. It's very cozy. All of my massage friends will be down there. We travel together and have a temple we set up for healing and massage."

"Sounds trippy. *Everything* here feels trippy after being away for so long. Back East it's all very matter of fact. There's no connection to nature. But not for nothing, I love it there. This has just been a strange trip. I'm feeling confused."

"Some asparagus will make you feel better," Pax said,

feeding me a stalk. He took the other end in his teeth and met my lips in the middle. I smiled, dancing off into the living room. I looked around and noticed that all the men were now trying to dress like Nico. They either wore skirts or sarongs. Irving stood in the far corner talking to a man I had never met before. Many faces seemed new, others were vaguely familiar, and still others, too familiar. I felt hurt by Irving's presence. There was a searing feeling through my chest and a weakness in my legs. Remembering him in my arms, remembering my innocence, the way I had loved him despite his distance, it was as though I never stopped.

I pretended to be having a good time, but kept glancing back. I couldn't make a move to say hello and Irving refused to look in my direction. The past became a dream that had never existed, and the nostalgia made me want to cry.

I walked away and through the kitchen without looking back. Diving into the empty bathroom, I pulled the sliding door closed, lifted up my dress and sat on the toilet. The red lighting gave my face a dark glow in the mirror above the sink. Vintage porn was pinned to the wall, and philodendrons crept across the ceiling ominously. A tear rolled down my cheek. I sat frozen, clasping my hands, staring blankly at the floor. I wanted to forget the abundance of love and pain flowing all through me. I flushed the toilet, shimmied my dress back down, washed my hands and smoothed my hair back. I opened the sliding door, and stepped out where another odd man was waiting to feed me.

"This is my first time ever wearing a skirt! What do you think?" he asked. He was tall with black hair and glasses, wearing a long shimmery skirt.

"I like it. Somehow, it suits you."

We talked for a while, and then with authority he said, "You won't be in New York for much longer. The community will find a way to bring you back to Seattle."

"Really."

"I know they will."

Overwhelmed, I descended the stairs and Nico's friend Nuri handed me a glass of absinthe. He frequently did business in New York and visited me there. We had a lot of fun hanging out with my friends, but it ended with one night of awkward lonely sex.

He now kissed me, trying to be smooth though I could sense his nervousness. I brushed his arm and tipped my glance sideways.

"Crazy party, isn't it?" he asked.

"Yes, it's a lot of fun," I said, drifting off towards Pax and his friends. He sat next to a bald man in a tunic with lotus flowers tattooed up his arms, and two fleshy girls with long hair and flowing dresses.

"Lauren, join us!"

I laughed light-heartedly and sat in the middle of the group.

"You are so beautiful," said the man in the tunic.

"Just sit back and relax," pitched in Pax.

"Wow, do any of you drink?" I asked, noting their empty hands.

"Oh no, not really."

"I sometimes fantasize about being that healthy, but it's never going to happen."

The four began to massage my arms and legs and I sank into the pillows. But I didn't want to be soothed, and was anxious to wander. I had to keep moving through rooms, through vibrant colors, past beautiful faces, in and out of conversations.

And then I was wasted and clutching a man from Rome who spoke little English. I didn't want him to speak. I didn't want him to have a mind, or any connection to me at all, beyond the physical. He was stunningly beautiful, and that was all I needed right then. I led him to the side of the house, and lifted his sarong, kneeling in front of him as he held my hair and I clung to his thighs.

"I don't care if anyone sees us," I said.

"We need to go in. No condom."

"That's okay."

"I safe."

"That's good!"

He looked down at me with his dark skin glowing, appearing as though he was chiseled from stone. He seemed more like a sex toy than a person. He pulled me up by the arms, and smoothed the sarong down. I came back to reality, and saw him from within. Minutes later we were in the bedroom full of people. We kissed under the covers, a tumble of limbs. Partygoers flew back and forth on the swing in gold vinyl and furry boots. Feathers and glitter left a trail behind them.

Hours passed, haze had prevailed and silence came. The sun was shining in through the window. I opened my eyes, disturbed by the light. I turned to the right where the man from Rome was sleeping heavily. I turned to the left where Nico was sprawled across the remaining edge of the bed.

"Whoa, what happened," I wondered quietly. Nico shifted in his sleep, and I realized that nothing more had happened than what I remembered.

Jo opened the door and walked in, "Wake up, we have to catch the boat to go up north!"

"What?" asked Nico. "Oh, I forgot! Oh Jo, you make me so horny," he said, pulling her down. He jumped up out of bed and ran around the room naked with a massive erection. Next to me, his friend rubbed his eyes and laughed.

"How stupid to take this trip the day after the party. It was crazy. We have to fit everything in for Maurizio though. Lauren, you were crazy last night," exclaimed Nico.

"I barely even remember what happened. One minute I was depressed and the next I was smashed."

"I remember!" spoke Maurizio, throwing up his hands and sitting straight up. Nico threw me a t-shirt and I pulled it over my head. I climbed the stairs and found my washed out reflection in the bathroom mirror. My head was pounding, and I needed a coffee.

Chapter 46

*"As such disappointments become more and more common,
sexual separatism commends itself as
the most plausible substitute for liberation."*

Christopher Lasch

Six months later, Pax arrived in New York to stay for a month. I was a little nervous to see him after so long, especially since we had only met once at the party. But he no longer had a residence and was living as a nomadic massage therapist wandering from city to city for an intriguing array of clients. He was planning to spend part of the time with me, and the rest with friends.

I was no longer dependent on anyone to give me life. I had more friends than I could count and ran into them wherever I went. The entire day from work to play was spent socializing. All that mattered to me now was friendship. Sometimes I would sleep with those friends, sometimes I would have feelings for those friends, but I was invulnerable to any sense of a relationship beyond that. It was a wonderful thing, to be so independent. Even the rare moment of loneliness was invigorating and wonderful to me, because in the city, life never stopped moving, and there was someone to talk to wherever I went.

I met up with Pax at a place in the Lower East Side and felt awkward at first. His energy was so strange and spiritual. He was staying at a hotel with his friend Michelle who was a famous porn star. She specialized in fire-play and could literally throw flames from her vagina. He often stayed with her family in Miami as their personal massage therapist. Her husband owned a successful strip club, where Pax massaged the dancers on breaks. Michelle traveled often for her expensive escort service.

Pax wanted to take me back to the hotel room so that he could give me a massage. I could see where this was going, and it was inevitable, since we would be sharing my bed for a couple of weeks. We took the subway, which spit us out into Times Square where masses of tourists jostled beneath bright lights that towered into the sky. In the sea of advertisements, it seemed the whole world was for sale. We rushed through the crush of people, and into the glass doors of the hotel. The hallways were black, and the room was tiny.

Pax set up his massage table, wedged into the only space available - the miniscule entrance of the room. Under the blanket on the table, I removed my clothes. Once settled, Pax's hands on my skin were feminine and light and I was drawn in, but nervous. I kept my eyes closed tightly in the headrest. It seemed that his arms were multiplying, that he was shape-shifting from the top of my head to the tip of my toes. I was certain he was removing his clothes, slowly taunting me.

But then Michelle burst through the door, waking me abruptly in her jumble of nerves. Sitting up, I saw that Pax was fully clothed, and I felt completely disoriented. Michelle apologized profusely for interrupting our moment. Her client had been too much, and she had to leave early. She was high on cocaine, fresh from some place in Jersey. She popped open her corset, freeing her enormous square shaped breasts. Then pulled down her pants revealing a g-string. Diving under the covers, she made herself as cozy and safe as possible. Her exhaustion beat out all the effects of the blow.

It was time to leave, so that Michelle could have a dark and restful quiet. I walked to the Path train feeling over-stimulated. I was relaxed from the massage, but my nerves were on edge. Fighting my way through overweight tourists taking pictures, I thought about how just being here was one of the big events of their lives. My life could have been just like theirs. I felt grateful, that it wasn't.

. . .

We were in Mid-town at the resident apartment of traveling Tantric Practitioners. Pax had taken me there me to visit two of his friends from Seattle. I sat on a hard wood floor, surrounded by towering red walls with a massive painting of an ancient couple in a tantric pose. Pax sat cross-legged next to me as Raven and Andrew worked in the kitchen. They were brewing mushroom tea. Raven was apparently a practitioner, and Andrew was an actor and a musician.

"We should take a walk through Central Park," said Andrew.

"As long as we can find our way back on that stuff," I laughed. I was the sole psilocybin virgin in the room, trying to uphold a semblance of bravery.

"At first you might feel nauseous, but it will pass. It helps to be outdoors, moving around. Your body will have a lot of energy to expel," Pax said, long white fingers folded in front of him.

Raven placed a mug in front of me. The mushrooms seemed so natural, and after living amidst cement and glass for so long, I craved nature. I stared at it for a moment as everyone else began drinking. Then I picked up the mug and took a sip. It tasted earthy and herbal, with a hint of honey.

"That's not bad," I said. Raven had a special recipe for making the tea less bitter.

We all quietly finished the brew and put on our coats. A strange silence came over the others that made me feel overly self-conscious. Pax and I descended the narrow staircase and waited in the cold as a wooden sign hanging from pegs blew in the wind above us.

"I feel strange," I said, as a wave of dizziness came over me and my stomach flip-flopped.

"That's normal," Pax replied.

"My stomach is churning."

"As soon as we walk, you'll feel better," he assured me.

Raven and Andrew tumbled out the door.

"Okay lets go," Andrew said, waving his hand forwards. He led the way down the street and we followed him as though he was our master.

The world became transformed with streams of endless light expanding into infinity. People were herding down the streets through black rainbow puddles of water, all flowing like liquid. I looked down at a dog that appeared to have no being within it, just a pile of black fluff quivering in a constant state of frenzy. It bothered me that the creature seemed so empty.

As we stood waiting at a crosswalk I turned to Pax and said, "Just be my reality okay?"

He smiled, looking far off to the other side of the street.

Behind us, Raven imparted, "That's one of the most beautiful things I've ever heard."

We began walking again and the streets grew dark. A man passed by with stiff posture and a thin straight line to his lips. I turned to Pax and claimed, "That man has killed several people."

He looked at me briefly with eyebrows raised.

The street grew light again and I felt life in my brown suede trench coat. I moved my hands in the pockets, making the coat billow in and out. "I'm wearing a cow!" I laughed. I could hear a distant 'moo' within it and began skipping forward, "Mooooo! Moo! Moo!"

A man on the corner spoke to us in a different language and Pax tried to respond, thinking he could speak the language fluently. Andrew took him by the elbow, "Sorry man, he's under the influence."

We walked through Columbus Circle where loud raucous marching band songs were playing at the entrance to the park.

"That sound is horrible! It's not music, it's propaganda!" I proclaimed, covering my ears.

"You're very perceptive," Raven said behind me.

As soon as we entered the trees and left the city, the nausea subsided. The ponds were composed of blue, gold, red and purple ringlets reflecting sparkling trees. We came to an empty stage where Pax walked within the dome, becoming darker as he descended into the shadows, and lighter as he stepped forward. I began to feel miles apart from all of them as they congregated together in front of the stage.

We meandered up the staircase behind the theater where a row of thick vine trees grew. I climbed up into a knotted tree and began to breathe in unison with the living wood. Beneath my hands the wood expanded up and down. I felt myself melding with the tree and memories of youth flooded back to me. Swallowed into magic, immersed in plants and animals, never wanting to leave for the world of people. I sat there, feeling found.

"We need to keep moving!" Pax's voice cut painfully through my core.

"No, I don't want to," I said flatly.

"We'll lose the others."

"But this is where I belong."

"Lauren."

I looked up, as though the sound of my name broke a spell. I clung tightly to the tree and then regretfully let go. I stood up, and tried to not look back as I slowly followed at a distance behind. We walked through a horse trainer's round, and then down some steps where Raven and Andrew were circling a statue that seemed to be mutating as we watched it. I stared as a stone squirrel turned into a panther. The woman at the top kept changing her expression.

We passed a skating rink where people circled in a herd

to more fake music. The scene was jarring and I felt sick again.

"I hate herds. People should never exceed groups of three or four."

The sound left us behind and church bells rang out, more crystal clear than anything I had ever heard. We soon came to a group of people roller-skating to disco music. Everyone was moving in different directions without the herd mentality. Each one stood out as an individual, almost alien and wonderfully diverse. The four of us stood watching, feeling exposed as we looked on, but wanting to join in the dancing.

"Won't they question us, staring at them like this?" I asked, nervously.

"Your sense of time is skewed. We've probably only been here for a second," said Pax, as his eyes followed the swirling roller skates.

"Lets move on," Andrew said.

As we neared the city, my stomach began to churn again. Pax, Raven, and Andrew stood staring up at the twinkling lights of skyscrapers, but I wanted to avoid the buildings. I was lost in the intricacy of a small tree, branches reaching out into a circle.

We were leaving plant life behind. City blocks flashed past with man-made light. Quickly we were back at the apartment where I felt lost among the humans. All of them were new to me. There was no one I could trust.

We settled in and removed our coats. I felt drawn to a vase full of red roses. I laid my head beneath them and watched as they moved to the sound of tinkling bells playing on a CD in the background.

"If you focus enough energy, you can open the roses," Pax said from somewhere behind me.

I focused my energy on a single rose and watched as it bent to my touch. I felt connected to the rose, but watched in disappointment as it began to wilt. "It's beginning to droop!"

"You're taking its energy. You need to give to it, rather than take away. Energy flows in a circle."

I focused again and watched as it slowly opened. The

thought entered me, that in prying for it's full beauty, I was also rushing the rose towards its eventual death.

"Come sit with us," Raven said from the couch. The three of them had gathered in a circle. I felt far away from them, and was afraid to join into their unit. I walked over and sat next to Raven on the couch.

"Lie back against my chest," she said, "I feel that you need to be nurtured. There's no need to separate yourself from people."

"It's easier to be alone," I laughed. Lying back against her, all I felt was fear. She was warm and seductive with slim arms that wrapped around me, stroking my skin. She was beautiful and it was some kind of trap. It all felt false. Her motive was to feel above me, as all women did. I was so tired of it. I counted the seconds before I could break away without offending her.

Finally I was back in my corner on the couch, half listening, half inside my mind. It became very hard to hear.

Pax was crying. "I dream that I'm dissecting bodies. I was a serial killer in a past life, and it completely disturbs me. But without that knowledge of the muscles, the structure of the human form, the nerves, I would not be a massage therapist. It's innate in me, this power to know so well how to ply the human form."

I didn't know what to do. I wanted to comfort him, but I was scared of him at the same time. I felt frozen, barely able to hear him at all. Eventually Pax took out a massage table. I wondered what sort of tantric sex acts took place on it. He gave Andrew a massage, and then expressed interest in doing some therapy on Raven. They straddled each other on the table. Apparently the work she needed was focused on her pelvic region.

Andrew and I became uncomfortable watching them. It felt intimate and strange. They were unnerved by our presence, and moved the table into the bedroom where they continued whatever it was they were doing in the dark. I sat on the couch, getting bored yet still feeling an adrenaline rush. Andrew suddenly had an enormous amount of energy to expel. He started manically cleaning the room, and then when there were no more pillows to put back in place, he started pacing. I didn't know what to say to him. We both felt jealous and estranged from the two people in the other room.

"I have to wake up early tomorrow!" Andrew yelled. There was no answer from the bedroom. " I think Lauren would like to be getting home. You'll miss the half hour train if you don't leave soon!" he called.

Home. Yes, I wanted to be home. What was home? Where was home? I wasn't sure. Suddenly I missed Seattle.

Chapter 47

*"They avoid close involvements,
which might release intense feelings of rage."*

Christopher Lasch

I was in a surreal world of Seattle faces gathered in a New York City apartment. It was Kara's place, a woman I had met years ago at Nico's. She had been the subject of a fight between Nico and I when he had posed nude with her for some strap-on pictures. And as I had suspected, she was not a showgirl in Vegas, but a sex worker running a successful brothel out of her place in the West Village.

Nico was on his way back from Italy, and was staying over for the weekend. Strangest of all, Aerin, the girl I'd seen Nico having sex with at Irving's party was now living on the Lower East Side. She had also dated Irving after I moved to New York and then moved a year after me.

I found it all so ironic. I had been at Kara's for an hour, and once again it was a competition for Nico's attention. He had decided against returning to Hoboken with me for the night because I had told him I didn't want to have sex.

Apparently this was the ultimate insult, especially since I said it in front of his friends. I no longer desired to be with him and he had no power over me. Though after all the intensity we had shared, friendship seemed slightly depressing. It was missing that essential element of passion that had always been between us.

Aerin won Nico for the night and they decided to go clubbing. She had already stuffed miniature bottles of vodka in the lining of her purse. I couldn't even afford to get into a club, and was not dressed for dancing with my bulky bag stuffed with clothes from work. No one else wanted to go. Kara and her friend felt too old for nightclubs. So I took the train back to my neighborhood where I could drink for almost nothing. No matter how many pours I had, the bartenders only charged me for one drink.

. . .

The next day I returned to Kara's apartment. Nico was in the bathroom taking a shower.

"So did they have sex," I asked.

"Yes. They woke me up at four in the morning. It was disrespectful. But you know, they were drunk and didn't know how loud they were. I didn't want her in my place. But where is she supposed to go with a kid and a boyfriend at home."

"I can't stand her. I find her repulsive."

"Not someone you can trust."

"Hello beautiful!" called Nico, walking down the hall.

"Hey!"

He kissed me and exclaimed, "I had so much fun last night! Aerin is still crazy!"

"I'm sure she is."

I wondered why I kept in touch with him at all. But then he hugged me, and I remembered how much I loved to be immersed in his lively energy. He strapped on his backpack and Kara picked up his other bag. We descended the narrow staircase and walked to the subway to take him to the airport.

Sitting on either side of him we both held his hands. People stared and wondered at the strange relationship. But I felt close with Kara through our shared experiences, while Nico felt distant. The trip took longer than expected and he kissed us goodbye, running to catch his plane.

When we got back from the subway, Kara took me to an expensive restaurant in Soho. I was so strapped I'd been living on lentil soup and tuna fish for a week. I felt out of place and strange sitting at a table in a corner where celebrities passed by, stoic and stick-like in their leather and long hair extensions.

We ate butterfish in a fava bean foam, beef carpaccio, and seared scallops on a bed of mache' with a bottle of champagne. I felt as though my company was being bought and sensed a deep well of loneliness within Kara.

"People are always taking advantage. Always," she complained, as the deep crease at the top of her nose became deeper.

"You know that crowd of healers in Seattle? Phillip, the one with the flower tattoos, and all of his friends?"

"Yeah, I met them at Nico's party last summer."

"Don't trust them. Phillip stole all this weed from me when I had a green house. He was always trying to get a free session from me. None of them have any money. So they just leach on."

"Well, I don't have money either, but I try not to leach," I laughed nervously.

"I can make you money."

"Oh, that's okay." I said, wondering about Kara's business of running a brothel from her apartment.

"I moved here for a man," Kara said abruptly, "When I got here he couldn't believe I came, and stopped talking to me. I live around the block from him, but I don't care. He had such dark energy. He was super into Aleister Crowley and all that. He worshipped Discordia, the goddess of chaos. Me, I don't believe in anything but touch. Touch is very healing. People need it. I'm in the business of touch, but no one is allowed to touch me back. That's what I miss the most. All that giving, but I long to receive it in my personal life.

"This girl Raven from that scene used to work for me, years ago. You know, as a prostitute. But she'll never say that's what she does now. None of them do. No way. Now they're all healers. She's a tantric practitioner. Whatever. Elevated term for a hooker. She completely betrayed me when she left. Thrives off of all those guys thinking she's some kind of goddess with special powers. She just needs to be wanted. By everyone."

"Yeah, I met her here through Pax."

Kara looked down into her purse, "Oh my goodness. I've missed a few calls! I turned the sound off. What if Nico's been calling us?"

"Oh no."

"I wonder if he missed his plane?"

She listened to the message, and quickly began to gather her things. "We have to go. He's been sitting on my doorstep for an hour in the freezing cold."

After she paid the bill, we rushed out, hailing a cab on Mercer Street in Soho. Back on Charles, Nico sat dejected and shivering on the staircase. "I missed my plane, man! And my phone died. I had to bribe people to use their phones."

I tried not to laugh.

We piled into the cozy building, cold and tired. Kara offered us her bed while she retired to the small room used for clients. Nico and I cuddled up under the dark red duvet while the cat slept at our feet. We looked into each other's eyes through the street light glow from the window above our heads. An air purifier hummed at the other end of the room, blurring the noise from the street outside.

"Lauren, I'm sorry I didn't go home with you last night."

"Oh, that's okay."

"You know, I love you."

"I love you too, Nico."

"Back when we were seeing each other, I stopped talking to you because I knew it was killing you. I wanted you to be strong and that's why I took myself out of your life for a while. I just wanted you to know that. I'm not a healthy man and I didn't want you to need me."

"I know Nico. I know that's why it had to end. I felt old for a year after that. I don't even know if I've let go of the experience of you yet."

"You don't have to. We'll always be friends."

"If you ever need anything Nico, I will be there for you."

Nico brushed his hand over my hair. He looked up out the window, "Look Lauren, it's snowing!"

"It always snows here!"

"Well, it's still beautiful."

"I'm glad we could have this night together."

"You know, watch out for Kara. She's crazy."

"I like her."

"Be careful."

"I miss you."

"I miss you too. Things aren't as fun as they used to be. Irving got married and has a kid and I have to keep him out of trouble when we go out. I don't see George as much. Colin moved to Vegas and is living with his Green Card wife. I guess everyone grew up, if that's what you call it."

"I don't think Aerin changed. I don't like her. I don't trust her either."

"You're holding the past against her Lauren. She's been through a lot."

"But I don't think she's a good person to be sleeping with. She's kind of a whore."

"You can talk. Sleeping with half of my friends, Lauren. I can't believe, Nuri too!"

"Oh come on, that was nothing," I waved my hand.

"You are still sensitive, no matter how thick your skin gets," he said.

"Why would that ever change?" I asked.

"Shhhh," he said putting his index finger to my lips, "It's too beautiful to be with you tonight. Lets not talk about depressing things."

Chapter 48

In my freshman year of college, my roommate never showed up. I had a dorm to myself, which was often good for getting work done, but was sometimes isolating. Prone to depression, loneliness was something I needed distance from.

In one of those dark moments, I felt the need to paint a portrait of my interior self. I tacked canvas to the wall. For accompaniment, I put the U2 song, "Jesus, Wake Up Dead Man" on repeat. The room was very dark, and I hardly remember actually painting. I went into some kind of trance.

In the painting I looked upward, completely barren with my arms wrapped around my own nakedness. It was all dark greens and sepia tones. Blood dripped down over my head and shoulders.

Coming out of the haze, I went to the communal bathroom to wash my brushes. A few girls stopped in afterwards and commented that they liked my painting. I didn't want to explain it to them.

I went to the end of the hall and told my friend about painting the depressing self-portrait. She said that I should go back into my room and pray. I went back, and closed the door. I took the painting off the wall and laid it on the dresser in front of the mirror. I stared at the reflection, and looked up at myself. But my eyes were completely empty in the mirror. Blank. There was nothing inside. My body was a shell and I was not in it. It scared me. I pricked my fingers with a needle to see if I could feel something. With the sting came spirits swarming above me in the tiny room. I started seething and my hands gripped around my neck. I threw myself down on the bed and hid my face in the pillow, praying for the spirits to leave, but it seemed I could never reach God.

I got up and tore the painting off the wall, throwing it out. Drifting in and out, I went to sleep two hours later. I was convinced that if I ever faltered again, the demons would come and take me for good. Everything outside of religion was dangerous. Every little thing could be the fall. As long as I kept praying, the spirits could never really reach me.

But what was worse – the fear of demons or the fear of God. The more I prayed the more strange things began to happen.

A very dynamic woman spoke at chapel. She challenged us all to pray for fifteen minutes a day for fifteen days to see just how much our lives would change for the good. I took her up on it and started going to the prayer chapel everyday. I followed the steps of prayer – praise, thanks, requests, and meditation. But the repetitions of my voice began to drive me crazy.

I told God that he was far above me when he already knew it. I thanked him for my family, my friends, and my life. I made selfish requests for boys to notice me, to have more friends, to get better grades. Then I would throw in an unselfish request for good measure. Something remote like orphans who needed homes, people who needed food, and those who needed saving. After that I would listen. I would listen for a long time. And soon I heard the Voice.

The Voice told me that there would be massive destruction and I would not be harmed. There would be great loss. In the vision that I saw, explosions burst out left and right. Buildings crumbled. I was scared shitless. Scared to be close to God and scared to be far away. It was a catch-22. I never fulfilled my fifteen days or prayed for fifteen minutes ever again. The demons went away. The visions went away. The useless words and prayers to a figure in my mind went away.

I realized that if you listened hard enough for voices, soon you would hear them. If you thought the spirits could overtake you, soon they really would. Religion mixed with imagination creates the most dangerous delusions.

Chapter 49

The next week Kara invited me over for dinner. She bought two decadent steaks and I sautéed them in butter. She was concerned by how thin I was and wanted to give me a meal rich in protein. It was one of the best steaks I'd ever had. After we ate, we settled in the living room and Kara shared her thoughts about the sex industry.

"I try to create a positive space for my customers, but it never works," she said, the deep crease between her brows sinking further in towards her skull. "It's never the guys. The girls are always flaky. With some of them, I'm lucky if they show up for work." She glared at the left corner of the room, somewhere beneath the bookshelf packed with books on women's lib and the sex trade. "I don't want to behave like their boss. I want them to feel cared for, but they take advantage. I'm just not tough enough."

"Managing them might help them feel a little more secure. It also gives the sense that you are in control."

"Maybe you're right, the girls really have no idea how much work and effort I put into this. They just show up and do their thing. You wouldn't believe how my most regular girl,

Angela raids the fridge and drinks all my wine. I leave it there for them, but there are limits to what kind of consumption I expect. She goes crazy, as though she can release all of her inhibitions and have a party when she's here. On top of that, she complains constantly about her soon to be ex-husband, and then talks too much to her clients after she's finished a session."

"Maybe you should start deducting the extra expenses from her percentage."

"You know, whenever I take a new girl on, they always betray me eventually. They go off, start their own business, and pretend I didn't teach them everything they know."

"Every beginner eventually wants the power to run the show. They don't see all that you do for them because you don't show them."

I looked around the room. The apartment was small, but very expensive. As though tongue in cheek, red lights were hung from the cabinets in the kitchen and a wall of bookshelves separated the tiny nook from the living room. Expensive stereo equipment took up one wall beneath the windows. Chinese lanterns hung from the ceiling, and the room was dominated by a large futon with silk throw pillows. The cats spent most of their time on a large climbing tree. To the right of the front door there was a small room for clients with a curtain in the hall that hid the rest of the apartment from view.

"I always say I'll leave the business, but then I'd be giving up the cause to legalize prostitution. My neighbors are so suspicious. The woman downstairs hates me. She looks at me as though I'm a plague that needs to be stamped out. Her husband is a little more curious about the whole thing."

I felt lucky. Of all of Nico's lovers, it seemed I had fared the best. Kara had told me the story of how she had moved in with Nico. They had been sleeping when a woman snuck in through the screen door and climbed into bed with them. Kara learned to go along with whatever happened, but she held it all against him.

After they broke up, she left teaching behind and became

a prostitute as a way to get back at Nico, but Kara hadn't counted on finding success. She started out at a sensual tanning salon where the Madame taught her how to give a man a happy ending without ever touching him. Soon Kara was adept at the same tricks, using her long hair to titillate the skin, wavering close enough to be electrifying over the outdated electronic music. Underneath neon bulbs, within the small room that falsely advertised the existence of tanning beds, she learned not to hate high heels, and soon gathered a strange collection of corsets and contraptions constructed entirely of silk and lace.

She went wherever the work took her. She never saved a penny, and couldn't equate where it all went, though she was soon making a minimum of three hundred dollars an hour, often upwards of eight hundred. It was never enough.

I wondered over our familiarity. As though we had known each other for years, when in reality we had just known the same *man* for years.

"He feels threatened by you," she said. "He has an issue with anyone who comes from money. And you're a stronger person now. He doesn't know how to take it. He doesn't know how to handle the fact that he can't control you anymore."

"Really?"

"Did he give you herpes?"

"Yes."

"He gives it to all of his favorite girls. He says that he wants to help people with their pain, but instead he takes pleasure in inflicting it. He wants others to feel the suffering that he's felt. I swear he does it on purpose."

"Maybe. But I don't like to place the blame on him. I allowed it to happen, as much as I regret having to deal with it now. It's hard to tell people, and sometimes I go into denial about it. I pretend it never happened and never say it to one-night stands. It makes me feel so guilty, but it's easier that way. Nico is more honest than I am."

"I know. Well it's very common. Most people don't even know that they are carriers."

Jazz played quietly through the air between us, easing

the awkward topic left behind. One of the cats jumped onto the futon and Kara stroked it's back and folded her legs up to her chest. She looked up, "You know, you should really observe a session sometime."

"I'm not interested."

"I could help you with your rent. You could make a thousand for observing three sessions. Men pay to have a girl watch, they like a voyeur. And you could see if you feel comfortable doing it yourself."

"No, I'm fine. My dad can get me out of a bind when it comes to money. I just hate asking him though, so I put it off too long. It's humiliating."

"Just let me know if you ever need help."

"Sure. You know. We're just not getting enough customers at the restaurant and the ones that show up are so cheap."

I tried to imagine what it would be like to observe a session. It bothered me that Kara had fallen into this way of life by playing the role of the victim. She really had no excuse. She'd been teaching English abroad and had a good education. But I could see she liked the excitement of living on the edge. Aiding men to live out their fantasies of submission, on constant beck and call.

A week later, Kara invited me over, but didn't tell me that business would be in session. Angela was there early for a client scheduled at 9pm. She sat on the futon and told me I had a lightness about me that New York had yet to take away. She seemed bitter, which was not surprising, since she was in the process of getting a divorce, taking care of two kids, going to nursing school, and working as a sex worker.

Her suitcase of lingerie was unpacked and spread across the kitchen table. She fingered each piece lovingly, fondling the silk and lace. She was a tall blonde, with a perfect body that she paraded around for us. Her naked breasts waited for her choice.

"What do you think?" she asked as she tried things on. She settled for pale pink with black lace, stilettos and thigh high stockings.

She disappeared behind the curtains that blocked the apartment from the front door and client room, and we heard the man arrive and go in. Kara didn't want me to leave until Angela was done with the session. Apparently we were just supposed to whisper and pretend we didn't exist in the back of the apartment. It was not good for conversation. On one hand there was the adrenaline of what was going on in the front room, and on the other was the immense boredom of waiting.

First the silence inspired my curiosity, but then Angela's distant voice started up and went on and on, continuing much past the time I would have liked to leave. I kept looking at my watch as once more the half hour train left the station. It seemed from what we could hear that Angela should have been paying the man to be her therapist, rather than have him pay for sex. Midnight was creeping up, and I wanted to get out of there. I felt trapped. Kara hadn't told me we'd be holed up here and it seemed like she was trying to trick me into living her life again.

"I really do have to go!" I burst out, as I bolted. Swooshing aside the curtain, I delicately tried to sneak out the front door. But the knob was stuck, and just then the John came out to leave as well, alarmed and unaware that anyone else had even been there.

"Oh my goodness!" he exclaimed, in surprise.

I panicked over the jammed door as Angela pushed him back into the room.

"Sorry," I called over my shoulder, escaping to freedom at last. I ran to the Christopher Street station to wait for the next train, laughing to myself at the look of shock on the guy's face. I wanted to understand the whole thing, but I couldn't. I couldn't understand why men were so afraid to be honest about what they really wanted in bed and why they chose to pay someone they weren't even allowed to touch. It seemed sterile, contrived and fake, a sale to fill an emotional need, the same as any other exchange. I grouped it with all the things people bought to fill the void in their lives; chocolate, decadent dinners, a bottle of wine, expensive clothing that feels like a warm embrace.

I couldn't deny that Angela was beautiful to look at in complex lingerie with garters and heels. It was worth paying just to see her beautiful body and snowy white skin framed artfully in expensive bits of fabric. But Kara had the plain appearance of a farmer's wife with pocked skin and deep creases through her face. She was too depressed to ever be truly sensual and carefree. How could one relax in her company? I couldn't even imagine Kara in heels because I'd only seen her in sweat suits, always hidden away and shapeless, within zippers and buttons, sweaters, coats and hats. It seemed that in her off time, Kara didn't want a soul to recognize that she ever *had* sex. I suppose men were drawn to Kara for her maternal nature, with the added power of her collection of much-used strap-ons.

Time passed and soon the pressure and stress of being around Kara became too much. Though we did interesting things together, I felt weighed down by her constant complaining and the ways that everyone had failed her. She took me to a sex worker's poetry reading where a lesbian acted out a scene on how she went from dressing as a man with breasts strapped down, to her transformation as a sexy, sensual stripper, complete with a strip-tease. The bartender seemed pissed off by the display of flesh or maybe the subject matter in general.

Then one time Kara asked if her friend Jerry could experience a girl's night with us. He was a father and husband who liked to cross-dress once a month and go out with other women. But I think I would have liked him better as a man since he barely talked at all and seemed disarmingly nervous. The whole night was boring, despite the game of watching people realize he wasn't what he appeared to be. That was the last time I went out with Kara. She had paid for our dinners and the cabs, and probably thought I was using her like everyone else at that point. Kara just never wanted to go to places I could actually afford, and never wanted to walk anywhere even if it was only five blocks.

In the end, we were supposed to meet up for coffee but Kara canceled so she could go see a client at a hotel in Times

Square. I was already in the city, on my way to meet her when she called.

"Are you sure you don't want to come and observe? It would be really great for you. I think you should come."

"Oh no, I'm fine. You know, still not interested. And you couldn't even pay me to go near Times Square."

"It's too bad. You could do so well at this. You have that intuition for people. I feel like it's such a waste."

"Well, it's not my thing. And I'm doing okay at the restaurant."

"I just don't know why you would prefer to waste your hours slaving away at that place."

"I have to go, but good luck with your session!"

"We'll talk soon!"

"Yeah, I have some free time in a few days."

But I never heard from her again. Years later, after I returned to Seattle, I saw her leaving a bar with a group of foreign men wearing suits. The moment passed so quickly, I couldn't find the words to say hello. She disappeared into a stretch limo, and I figured Kara wouldn't respond if there were clients around. But still it made me feel incredibly sad, because I had loved her, and maybe loved the person she could have been, or once was. She was "empowered," but lost family and friends, hid from the law, lied to the neighbors, and lived in secret. An isolated life, imbalanced from too much giving. She had given so much, and received so little. You could feel the rage bottled up within her. It depressed me completely.

Chapter 50

When I was nine my parents shipped me off for my first solo trip – a week at the grandparents. There was nothing to do. My grandpa played cards with me and smoked his pipe. My grandma stayed on the periphery. I was afraid of her. I had no reason to be, but I'd had a nightmare where she yelled at me and threw a gift I gave her on the ground. "It's not good enough!" she screamed. Maybe she had treated her own children this way, but never me.

With me, she wanted to give me everything that my mom wouldn't. There were no well-balanced meals. She took me into the kitchen and like Vanna White, waved her hand across a wide array of pastries and sugar delights. I spent the next two days on the toilet with diarrhea. At bedtime, I cried myself to sleep. I never wanted to be separated from my parents ever again. Grandma and grandpa's house felt like a boring, sugar-ridden nightmare with endless games of cards.

The next morning I asked if I could go home early. I had never felt that depressed before. They called my parents and took me to McDonald's, where I actually ordered a salad. My parents came to pick me up and on the drive home my dad called to the backseat, "We made a decision while you were away."

"Okay?"

"We've decided to accept a job offer I have in Seattle. Your sister and I are moving there in September so I can start and she can be there for the whole school year. You and mom will stay here to sell the house."

"You're just moving without asking me first? What if I don't want to leave?"

"Well, this is what we're doing. You might not like it now, but you'll see, it will be fine."

A month later my dad and sister were gone, living in an apartment and looking for a house. They promised they would find one twice the size of our small ranch. But things weren't going so well on our end. We were both constantly sick, and I missed my dad and sister so much it was painful. The pain was like something tearing through my chest. I had temper tantrums more suited to a child much younger than I was. I remember screaming and flailing on my sister's beanbag as my mom tried to talk to them on the phone.

That October, my grandmother, a diabetic with depression, had five heart attacks in a row and didn't make it through the fifth. For the funeral, they had to pin her heart down in her chest because it was bulging so terribly. My youngest cousin screamed all through the service because he was convinced that she was going to sit up in her open casket. The Catholic ritual of kissing the dead body disturbed my mother. "She's not in there anymore," she said. "I don't want to remember her this way."

I gazed at the body that now looked like stone, then quickly looked away, trying to forget. It was a relief when afterwards, the old ladies of the church laid out a spread of food on picnic tables behind the house. Potato salad and bean salad and noodle salad and rolls. My mother gave me a stuffed mouse that had been in the hospital room with my grandmother. I didn't want to touch it. If I touched it, I would be touching death. I would be touching her corpse. I couldn't wait for an excuse to give it to the Salvation Army, without hurting her feelings.

On that day, my mother became the child. She could not be alone at night. She was too afraid of all the spirits. Every night we either packed our bags to stay at her friend's house, or a friend came and stayed with us.

I was shocked to find a bottle of liquor hidden in the back of the fridge. My mom had never even had a glass of wine since she'd been "saved." I had always been told that liquor turns you into a monster. Drinking was a sin. I was afraid that I would see her take a sip, afraid of what she could become.

Before all this my mom had been a distant maternal goddess who took care of all my needs. But now I saw that she was weak and helpless. I had to be the strong one now. And it made me angry. I hated women for not being self-sufficient – for always needing a man or a mother or a God. I hated that she needed to be so protected, like a child. Her reality was built on sticks that could collapse at any moment.

I lashed out at my mother's weakness whenever I had the chance. I even attacked her friend that stayed with us. I made my mother cry. But at least with me, she was not alone.

Chapter 51

Pax took me to see the guy he was now staying with, David Kane, who was something of a personality as an editor at a marijuana magazine.

"So David is Wiccan. Just to let you know, his place is pretty intense. I think you'll find him entertaining."

We took the elevator up the cliff from the backside of Hoboken and made our way through an excess of children running around. Walking around the bend, the wind whipped up from the side of the cliff, and we could see across Manhattan. The street seemed ominous as we approached David's building, and a thick energy hung in the air. We entered the front hall, and the place looked as though it had once been a funeral home. The ceilings were so high, it was unnerving, and the carpet hadn't been changed since the seventies. Austere, dusty flower arrangements sat on tables placed on either side of the stairwell.

It was right about then that I felt a bit nervous. I pictured some dark goateed character with a cape, sitting on a throne ensconced in red velvet curtains, drinking from a silver goblet. But what we found behind the apartment door was a jovial rocker, short of stature but huge on personality. He had long brown hair, and did actually have a goatee, but that was as far as it went. His smile was full of warmth, and his eyes twinkled with excitement over his many passions that he passed on to us in an endless game of show and tell.

The walls were covered with rock posters, mostly vintage Led Zeppelin and Ozzy Osborne. Everywhere there was memorabilia and nifty items that marked the history of his life. Surrounding the fireplace was a massive sound system, and overhead a large flat screen TV. An action figure, Loki (the Norse god of mischief), had its own altar set up in the corner. As a follower, David embraced chaos and anarchy.

I climbed up into the loft over the kitchen and looked down at Pax and David. There were so many things to look at. I felt over-stimulated, and wanted to read the titles of every book on the shelves and touch every exotic thing lying around. A black cat named Yang played with a bottle cap. David informed us that Yang's pure white sister, Ying had passed away a few months ago.

The height of the loft made me feel unsteady, so I climbed down the ladder. David lit a small Palo Santo wood chip and the smoke filled the room with a rich scent similar to frankincense. "This cleanses the air," he said. He showed us some of his favorite film clips, and laughed over his obsessed online fans, bemoaning the fact that most of them were unattractive and well past their prime.

David confessed how nervous he became over appearances for the magazine. He demonstrated his Jim Morrison strut, with the addition of aviator sunglasses that he never removed in public. Underneath his mask he was shy and insecure but extremely intelligent.

In some respects, David reminded me of Nico. He had the charisma of a celebrity. His lair was a crazy extension of all the things he loved. The main difference was that David was rather awkward around women, and had a hard time looking me in the eye. The most famous people I have known have also been the most awkward. They live with two personas -

the person they really are, and the person they pretend to be.

A week later, Pax brought my friends and I to David's annual Saturnalia party. There were only a few of us there who weren't members of the Coven, and David greeted us warmly in a crimson toga and a large gold studded belt cinched at the waist. David's energy was running rampant and he was thrilled to be bringing an ancient Roman holiday to his friends. The coven was not quite what I had expected. The group was comprised of older women with thick Jersey accents and gay men. In fact, David was the only straight male in the group.

The high priestess, Lady Gwendolyn was to lead a ritual at midnight. She looked comforting and motherly with big hair and large round rose tinted glasses. She entered the living room with her daughter who also seemed very maternal. If we had been on the west coast, all of these women would have had flowing skirts, long unkempt hair, and chunky jewelry; but not here. These women were just from the neighborhood and had no airs about tending to tree gnomes in mystical forests.

Within the coven there was a firm hierarchy of levels and obedience. Knowledge was revealed only after years of discipline. David's master was Darin who was known within the Coven as Lord Guidylon, a gay Latino man with glasses and a goatee. Darin seemed calm at the moment, but I had heard stories from Pax of his electrical energy field and persistent need for chaos. Strange events often occurred in one place while he had moved on to the next.

I wondered what my mother would think if she knew I was here. I thought of her friend the ex-wiccan who became a control freak Christian, and how I had been spanked for asking what the word "witch" meant. I realized, that my mother had never really known the answer to that question.

I watched as the high priestess approached Darin, "It will be an auspicious night for the ceremony. Have you seen the moon? Crystal clear tonight with such a bite in the air."

They moved to the hallway where they spoke in hushed voices. Then she returned and set an altar with burgundy velvet embroidered with silver. Over this she placed boughs of cedar and frankincense and represented the four elements with water, feathers for air, salt for earth, and a candle for fire. Candles were lit throughout the room. At midnight the lights were turned out and Lady Gwendolyn's voice boomed with authority.

"It is time to cast the circle. If any of you are not comfortable with participating you may step back now. Once the circle is cast, it will not be broken."

My friends moved back towards the kitchen where they giggled from too many pot brownies. Everyone else stood around the living room and joined hands, and I silently joined the circle.

"Face the east and breathe in."

Tendrils of smoke from incense and sage gave the air a pungent thickness. The members of the coven turned and brought in a deep breath followed by guests who were uncertain as to which direction to turn.

"Now face to the west."

Everyone pivoted. David's eyes were filled with the flame of the candle in front of him. Ferrell stood next to him, a gay witch with a soft voice and stoned half moon eyes. He sighed contentedly.

"Lord Guidylon, come forward," spoke the high priestess.

Darin laughed, "I knew I would be chosen." Walking towards her he held the handle of his athame to his forehead. The blade curved down in an S shape and caught the light. He stood in front of Lady Gwendolyn as she lifted a silver chalice of wine into the air.

"This wine represents the eternal mother. It is the darkness of the womb, the darkness that we represent and the light that we come out into." Silence hung softly for a moment. She closed her eyes and then opened them again.

"Lord Guidylon. Dip your athame into the cup and experience its life force."

He stepped towards her. His black curls glowed in the dim light. Holding his dagger between his two hands in reverence, he dipped it down into the chalice and turned it in a circle through the glass. He lifted the dagger up and held it to his heart. She turned and set the cup down on the table next to a round cake.

"This is the Yule cake. In the ancient Roman tradition there is a pea and a bean concealed inside the cake. The woman who gets the pea will be named the Lady of Misrule. The man who finds the bean will be the Lord of Misrule. If a woman gets the bean or vice versa, they will choose the Lord or Lady. As the jesters, they must do whatever they are told for the remainder of the evening.

Ferrell passed out the cake. He took the last piece and promptly bit into the bean. "I knew it! And I passed out the entire cake specifically not to get the bean."

Everyone nibbled happily, and no one really asked the Lord and Lady to do anything out of the ordinary. David sat on the easy chair, draped in his toga like a king on his throne. His legs were crossed, and he held his wine in his left hand. Everyone seemed content, and the room felt festive. Darin turned up some music and we all started dancing. The night turned into a typical party, without a sign that a ritual had just taken place. Some raucous, loud friends showed up, spoiling the mood, and soon the night was ending, as witch-by-witch slowly disappeared into the night.

Chapter 52

After three years of living in Hoboken, I grew tired of the constant struggle to get by, and Seattle was calling me home. Pax helped me move back to Seattle with my two cats. I returned, broke as usual, to my parent's house, but they were not living in it at the time. My mother's passion for Italian culture had grown, and they had been offered a position to live in Perugia, Italy for a year where my father could help grow a manufacturing site for the European market. He had always been an engineer, designing lifts for construction and entertainment, but now he was busy managing people and the business.

I had spent two weeks with them in December, living in their expansive villa paid for by the company, with an entire wing all to myself. My mother spoke Italian fluently now, and I practiced the bits I remembered from our classes at the supermarket or in town. My parents were more relaxed and happy than they had ever been. Suddenly they understood that life should be enjoyed.

With Pax gone, I was alone in their house, and I savored

the quiet. In the mornings, the hot showers seemed like a gift. In the afternoons, I spent three hours a day weeding the over-run garden. The weeds were all three feet high, with blackberry vines choking the trees. The caretakers had run out three months before I returned. Every night I built fires in the fireplace, made luxurious meals, and fell into the comforts of home with Gucci and Valentino on the couch. I hadn't watched television in three years, and I didn't mind living vicariously through characters on the screen after living so much, myself.

When the moving truck finally arrived with my crate of furniture and books, the neighbors called the cops. They thought someone had hired a truck to steal all of my parent's stuff while they were gone. I wasn't used to such watchful eyes, but it was good to know that people were looking out for them.

Pax was still homeless and living as a nomad, always returning with weird stories and strange drugs. One night, we ate some shroom chocolate, took a bath and came downstairs to sit on the big leather couches.

"Your energy seems blocked off to me," Pax said, lying back relaxed.

"Well right now my energy is blocked off to everyone who wants something from me. If you'd just let me be, maybe I'd open up to you," I replied, in reclusive mode.

"I do," he insisted.

"Sometimes."

"You always sit so far away from me. Why don't you come closer? You block yourself off from touch when it can be healing."

I moved to the large couch across from Pax, and hugged my knees. "You're right. I'm sorry I seem far away. Can't help it. I'm just shy or something, or afraid to be close to anyone. You can blame all the men in the world. I've loved them, but they've never been able to love me back." I felt pathetic, just then. To make up for it, I got up and laid down on Pax with my back to his chest. He wrapped his pale arms around me.

"You know, I don't feel anything yet," I said, referring to

the magic chocolate.

"You will. It takes time." He inhaled deeply, spreading his ribs wide up towards my back and breathing out. His heart was suddenly pounding up into my body. I felt his blood coursing rhythmically, massaging my body up and down.

"I think your blood vessels are giving me a massage! I can feel them all through me!" I exclaimed.

"I *am* massage," he stated, like a Zen master.

"That's crazy. I can't believe you aren't even aware that it's happening. Can't you feel it?"

"No."

I said nothing for a few passing minutes, feeling the blood flow through its course. But soon my mind drifted. I was overwhelmed with loneliness and the otherworldly being beneath me. I quickly stood up, and my head was spinning.

"Whoa. Take it slow," he said, sitting up.

"Oh my goodness!" I said, holding my head.

"Yeah, slow movements," he reminded.

"I can't sit down. I have too much energy," I said, shaking my hands.

Pax smiled up at me. His crystalline blue eyes watered behind studious looking spectacles. My cats came running up to us and I was shocked by their appearance. They appeared fluffy and out of control with wild long faces.

"Why are they following me?" I asked.

"Because you feed them."

I hated when people assumed my cats only loved me for the food.

"Why do they want to be around me?" I asked.

"They love you." This was a more satisfying answer. I smiled at them. Yet I couldn't see into them the way I normally could, and no matter how far I reached, I wouldn't be able to reach them.

"They look so ridiculous and strange. I can't even tell them apart!"

"Well, they *were* in the womb together."

"Yes. They are playing tricks on me, switching bodies or something. They think it's funny, but it's not. It really bothers me. Tell them to stop!" I exclaimed, as I paced in circles and figure eights.

"Stop," he said.

"They won't stop." I shook my head.

"No. You need to stop. They won't stop until you do," he reasoned.

"But the energy won't contain itself in me."

"It's moving through your system. And you're trying to avoid me. You're shutting down. Come to the bedroom," he suggested.

I glanced at him. His skin glowed and the flawless angles of his face appealed to me. My eyebrows pressed against each other as I tried to solve his methods. I didn't like to be directed. We went downstairs, and I fell back against the bed.

"I don't think I'll ever be able to sit up again. There is so much weight in me. I feel so heavy. I must weigh over a hundred pounds," I laughed.

He smiled. "You will let it go soon. You've blocked everything out for so long you've become repressed and weighty. You carry too much."

Massage therapists are so good at making you feel that you're broken and need to be fixed. Lying next to me, Pax kissed my cheek and ran his long manicured fingers through my hair. He took his glasses off and set them on the shelf next to the bed. We kissed, but his persistence was annoying. I felt him pressing towards sex, but everything in the room tantalized and stimulated my senses far more than he could. The music he had turned on was so distracting - a ceaseless chanting, with jungle drums that caused masses of dark green foliage to spring up all around us with disarming root structures spreading tentacles into the carpet wriggling with life. Humid wetness was seeping into me and the weight of the air was overwhelming. He was fingering me now, but it was taking place miles away. It was as though I only existed inside my mind. I felt detached from my body completely.

"I can't take this!" I started laughing hysterically. "I'm so lost in the jungle. Get me out!"

"The jungle?" he asked.

"The music, you have to change the music."

"Okay." He walked off towards the stereo.

"But don't take too long!" I was afraid he would disappear and I would be alone again. But magically he reemerged, a different song starting up behind him.

"No, we're still in the jungle," I complained.

"Half of my music is in the jungle!"

"I know, mine too!" Fits of laughter spilled out of us and we felt we would never be able to swallow it up again. I buried my face in the pillow feeling embarrassed by the mass of emotions I could not control.

"How about jazz?"

"Remind me, what is jazz again? That sounds so good though. I can't think in categories anymore. It's so strange! They're slipping away. Except for the jungle. I think I ate too much of the fungi chocolate. It shouldn't be disguised in something so delicious!"

"Just don't let it get on top of you, because I want to instead," he joked.

"The drugs or you. Hmm. Yes, I'd like you on top of me too."

The stereo began to spill out the chords of "Body and Soul." He kissed me again. I closed my eyes, but every time I did, I drifted away into Billie Holiday's voice. I had lived through this music. I knew I had. Turning away, tears formed at the corners of my eyes and fell down my face as I thought of all the innocence I had lost along the way, though I wasn't sure exactly what innocence was to begin with. I then realized that Pax was looking down at me, wondering where I had gone.

"I was supposed to be kissing you, but the music took me away again. I don't think we can listen to it!"

"No problem."

He walked away and switched off my childhood with a button. Lying down again he started up where he had left off, which kept making me feel like a fish. The sounds of water filled my ears and energy rushed through my body, like waves coursing up and down. But his touch was so far away from my head where I chose to reside. I started to contemplate my breathing. How many breaths had I taken in this life? And how many more? What if I stopped? The thought of stopping sounded like a great relief. All those breaths were so much work and effort and it was all very exhausting.

In the same way that I must have seemed so far away from Pax, he always seemed faraway to me. I decided he was lost somewhere in his ego. Before the move, he had made some odd confessions and told me that he was God. It was a concept difficult to comprehend, being unfamiliar with eastern thought.

"I am God. How could I not be? I willed myself into existence. My mother was on the table, about to abort me, and I changed her mind. She had to force my father to meet me. It took him weeks before he could face the truth. When I was older I could see inside of people. In a past life I dissected humans. But you know, I take energy to keep on living. I have this disease where I age in the sun, but I keep riding the waves of other people. Like surfing on their life force. It's a slippery slope. You have to be careful to keep them from finding out you are a vampire."

"You weren't careful with me," I said, uncertainly.

"I know you are stronger than the rest. Your life force is powerful. You can handle it, and you will find the energy to replace the energy that I took. That is why I can be with you for such extended periods of time."

"How do I replace it?" I asked.

"Don't you see? You magnetize energy."

"Well, I like being around you. I've gotten so used to you being in my apartment. I just don't know how long I can afford to feed us both. Energetically and physically I guess."

I wasn't sure why I slept with him when I never felt the currents of expectancy, never really anticipated his arrival, never let him inside my fantasies, and never felt quite present when he was making love to me. Where was he ever? Like a spirit moving through rooms and buildings and cities. It was easy to let him stay, floating through my life with little effect on my emotions. I was in love with someone else in an entirely different city, which kept me invulnerable to everyone that was actually knocking on my door. I still don't know if Pax had feelings for me; he was so quiet, it was impossible to tell.

"I am God," he would say. And then later on, "I don't believe in God or Satan."

"Then how could you be God?" I teased.

"I am God of my own existence, and so are you," he said, pointing at me.

"The mind is a powerful thing, but mind control won't make you immortal."

"My spirit is immortal," he replied.

"I give up with you. You're such an odd duck."

"Quack."

I was exhausted and energized by him all at once. In New York City we had walked down grey winter city streets. I watched him step lightly as though he was made of glass. He wore vintage war coats that were too large for him while I wore faux fur and a chapeau. I was consumed with the theatrical image we must have cast. Two lost souls walking off the film set, not certain where to go.

Usually he was high, which I thought of as a longing for relief from all the energy he'd sucked. In the bedroom he appeared to be like a woman with no hair and a penis. Every other week he would grow out his hair and goatee, and then shave it again. With hair he looked rather masculine, with the gaunt features of an ex-convict. But then the glasses made him appear studious, like he should be reading in a coffee shop. In the mornings, sitting on the rug in meditation, he rolled his eyes back into his head, demonic looking and strange.

Wandering through the country he networked and shared his gift of touch. When homeless people asked for money, he explained to them that he was homeless too. He lived off the generosity of others, and knew that it probably wouldn't last forever. As a child, he said his mother had stolen his identity and put him in massive credit card debt before the age of ten. Apparently identity theft is most common within families. He never sought to fix the bad credit, or take his own mother to court. Instead he lived under the grid, never renting a place in his name, living quietly with others. Leaching money and energy, hiding from the sun, racing against the grey hair and pale skin at the age of thirty-four, and the bones in his body that were already failing to hold him up properly.

In New Jersey I had become a stronger, happier person surrounded by amazing friends. But in the process, I avoided healing from past issues named Irving, Nico, and so on. Pax seemed like some kind of remedy. Through massage and touch he could work out the negative feelings I held within my body. But instead, he led me right back to the source.

Chapter 53

Two months later I had dinner at Nico's house. I was in the same kitchen chair I had always sat in, while Nico was at the head of the table. His friend, Charlotte, was also there. She began to massage his shoulders.

"You know, all this time you've never once come in for a massage from me. I want to give you a massage on Tuesday for your back pain, one on Friday to ease your tension, one for fun. Why don't you come in?" she asked.

"I don't know," he said, shrugging.

Abruptly she added, "Oh, I would've proposed to you a long time ago, if only you could be monogamous." She flipped her hair, and looked up at the ceiling. She was tall and plain, with limp hair and glasses.

I smirked, and took a sip of the too-sweet wine, to hide my reaction.

"It's too bad we can't be together," Charlotte rambled on, as though I wasn't in the room. Her kneading hands were determined to claim Nico as her territory.

"How do you know Nico?" she asked, turning to me.

Before I could respond, Nico answered forcefully, "We dated a long time ago."

"We've known each other for six years," I added.

I saw the defeat in Charlotte's face and sat contemplating why every woman had to feel that she was the one who would make Nico forget all the others. Unnerved by my quiet stoicism, Charlotte became more determined to vocalize her place in Nico's life.

"You know Nico, you are so good at finding cheap tickets to Italy, you really must find one for me to South Africa. They're ridiculously expensive. And I want to fly home for the holidays."

She paused, and turned, noticing that the cat had come in, "Oh it's Oofa! Ti amo gatto! I really am going to take him home with me one of these days and make him mine."

"What have you been up to Lauren?" Nico asked, grateful for a break from her prodding.

"I spend all my free time writing now. After so many years of partying, I've gotten a little reclusive. But it feels good."

"I'm bored with partying," Nico said, getting up from the table. "You know, I stopped smoking! Three months now. I haven't had a drink in twenty-one days."

"Are you counting the days until you start again?" I asked.

He glazed over at my comment. "People keep wondering why I don't show up to events so much. There's more to life. I feel it will soon be time for me to leave." he said, solemnly.

"No, there's no reason to leave. All your friends are here," Charlotte moaned.

"I want to be alone with my thoughts," he replied. "It's the only way that I can grow."

"I want to just be," I responded. "To just be everything that pertains to the moment. Nothing else wasting my time."

Charlotte squinted her eyes at me through her slim glasses.

I glanced at my watch, "Well, it's getting late. I should be going."

"No, don't go Lauren. Stay the night?" Nico asked.

"No. It's time for me to leave." I got up from my chair. Charlotte stayed in the kitchen as Nico came bounding up behind me.

"I love you, Lauren."

"I love you too Nico. I have a feeling I won't be seeing you for a long time. But, you'll always be with me in spirit."

"You too. There's no one else like you."

I slipped on my shoes. He kissed me, and I walked out the front door, turning back to wave through the mish-mash of Italian replica sculptures on the porch. Leaning up against the doorframe, his bearded face was rugged with crow's feet crinkling around his eyes, skin the color of clay. The light from inside the house cast a glow all around him - like Zeus among the gods.

Chapter 54

*"Eventually we came to accept the lying and the role-playing
and the compromises so completely
that they were invisible – even to ourselves."*

Erica Jong

I was at a local Burning Man retreat. The camp was
muddy, with pools the color of defecation. The continual
drizzle dissuaded constant displays of flesh - pasty white, and
dimpled. I felt trapped in my tent where my clothes and
bedding smelled of damp mustiness and dragged-in grass. If I
stepped out I would have to converse with people I didn't
know. And since I didn't want to tell anyone how terrible I
felt, I could barely talk at all.

Pax had invited me, and we had planned on camping
together. He came early, since I could only stay for the
weekend. But when I arrived, he seemed afraid, cowering as
he spoke, looking for the quickest escape. He led me to my
tent that he'd brought with him.

"There's nothing in it. Where's all your stuff?" I asked.

"I just put the tent up yesterday," he replied. Even then I

thought he must have slept in the community tent. But his new friend Emily had driven him in at the beginning of the week. Emily was a dominatrix he had met at a club a month ago.

"If you need help unloading your stuff, just ask someone. But Lauren, you need to ask," he said, as though I had an inability to delegate.

Of course, after he left me there, I unloaded everything by myself.

An older, over-weight blonde woman appeared by my car. "Are you going to be there for long?" she asked, in a bad mood.

"No. Just two more trips," I said cheerfully, deflecting her glare.

"Good. I'll stand here and wait then. I mean, unless I can drive up now."

"Well, there wouldn't be a way for me to get out then," I replied.

"Okay. So that's an issue," she said, folding her arms across her chest.

I was annoyed. My first interaction with a stranger in the camp was not promising. Furthermore, the woman would be camping right next to me. After I finished, Pax rushed around helping the woman get her tent up while I felt invisible. He avoided looking me in the eye, and kept his body turned away from me.

Alone, inside my tent, Pax took over my mind, sneaking around in ways I found disturbing. Then the orgasmic moans began, becoming louder and more melodramatic as the seconds ticked by. I was certain that it was Emily. I pictured her, beautiful in a sensitive way with long black hair and a massive stark white rump that she paraded around in thongs, crazy bondage gear, and high heels. The loud, persistent moans (which seemed like they were just for show), made me feel inadequate. But later that day, as I sat in a chair by the communal kitchen, Emily was the first person to smile at me.

Pax eventually mentioned that he was having sex with Emily. He wrote it off as therapy. She allowed him to be more aggressive. He claimed that all of his previous lovers had been too damaged to allow him to be his true self. With me, he had always been uncertain, asking for direction, when I just wanted him to take charge. He could hardly accept the fact that he had a penis and told me that he wished he didn't have one.

That night I felt like a fake, donning my old gear from the Nico days. Pax got lost in the crowd, jealous as I talked to an aging hippy at the bar. So I wandered to the empty dance floor. The DJ spun his records and I danced to forget where I was. After a few songs, the dance floor was packed.

A woman complimented my dance moves. She tried to tell me what to do, pursuing me solely for the power trip. When she invited me to her tent, arms groping about my waist, I broke away and disappeared into the darkness behind some trees. Eventually, she trudged away with friends.

I went back to camp and wondered if everyone would get laid tonight except for me. I wanted to get off the bus. This was not my life anymore. No one could make me drink the kool-aid, and I had outgrown the trip.

In the morning I wandered around, then sat in the massage tent and watched a row of people getting rubdowns.

"Can I touch you?" asked the leader of the camp. His girlfriend stood stirring beans across the way in the kitchen.

"Yes."

"I'm one of the few people in this camp who is not trained in massage. But I've been told I have a knack. He pressed his fingers beneath the tight muscles in my shoulders. I breathed deeply. I had not been touched in a long time. His hands ran up and down my arms and across my shoulders.

"Can I kiss you?"

"Yes."

His lips brushed mine and his girlfriend smiled at me from a distance. She wore a straw hat and overalls with nothing underneath. A large bumbly breast poked out from the side.

I stood up silently, and left them all, making my way down to the river. I took off all my clothes and sat on a huge log with a towering root structure and large branches.

Swallows swooped over the rapids, daring the water to catch them. I began to meditate, and my body felt open. No longer limited by the physical world, I was weightless and free from the human chain.

I wanted to stay in that place forever, relieved from all my thoughts. But instead, I dressed and began to walk back to the camp, passing a wiry man with a grey beard who wore a super hero helmet made out of papier-mâché.

As I entered the common area, I heard loud whacks and sharp cries. A man was strapped to a large black web tied up between two trees. The woman who was camping next to me was spilling out of a miniscule black vinyl costume with a large whip and an assortment of other devices set up on the grass.

Everyone stood around watching in costumes they hoped would not be out-done. They were unattractive in their desperation for attention. Their fizzled minds were lost on drugs. The air was heavy with the stench of un-bathed bodies that had fornicated in rain and mud. I surveyed the sagging breasts, pinched in fat, and the straps that squeezed it all in so tightly.

A thud hit the bottom of my stomach. Nauseous, I ran for the nearest port-o-potty. It didn't matter to me that shit was smeared across the floor. It was my only haven. I decided that I would pack my things and go. I was done with all of it, the whole pathetic scene. I threw open the door of the port-o-potty and marched to my tent. Nothing could stop me from driving away, out the front gate.

No one took notice as I dismantled the tent and stuffed my belongings into the back of the car. At the last minute, the man who had kissed me came running, and asked if everything was okay. I told him that it was a long story. It was a story that had started a long time ago, and here I still was. He asked if the bondage play had bothered me. I told him, that no, I had seen it all before. It wasn't *what* they did. It was *why* they did it. It was sad that they had to try that hard just to feel something. Or maybe they felt too much, and the physical pain could erase the emotional pain. And I was twenty-one again, in the counselor's office, being handed a list called "Things That Make Me Happy." But I just wasn't broken anymore.

Chapter 55

Out of all the people I knew through Nico, Colin was the last person I thought would die young. Life is never what you expect. It was painful to watch the slideshow of him at his sending off party at Nico's house. At first, he was a beautiful young man so full of life and curiosity. By the end, he was slumped over in a chair barely able to hold up his head, hidden behind sunglasses and layers of clothes, cancer-ridden. He was only 39 years old.

His death is a deep pain within my gut. I hear his voice reminding me that life is short and if we don't share our stories, they will slip away and disappear. Moments pass, people pass, our own lives pass us by so fast, we catch ourselves grasping backwards to hold on.

In the living room, I was surrounded by people I once found intimidating, but now found myself relating to. Everyone took turns sharing how they lost their virginity. I heard a trail of echoes across the room.

"I was twenty-one."

"Twenty-one, too. I was an adult then," said Jo.

"Twenty-three and I was engaged. It felt simple. Nothing

seemed to fit before. I was Seventh Day Adventist."

"I was the pastor's son, Seventh Day Adventist, too. But I was only sixteen. I went to a camp and was planning to have sex, but the counselors confiscated my condoms and expelled me. Back home I snuck out to a kegger. There were five of us guys sitting in a row. The girls were all across the way. One of the guys wasn't a virgin. He turned to us and said, 'See that girl over there? By the end of the night she'll have slept with all of us.' We all turned to each other and said, 'No way.' He walked over to her, said a few words and they disappeared into the woods. When they came back he walked her over to the next guy and placed the girl's hand on his arm. She took us *all* into the woods that night."

Earlier on, I talked to Nico's housemate, who was an expert in Chinese medicine. I told him how I believe that depression is a direct result of repressing our emotions. He replied, "That makes sense. What is the natural reaction to repression? The pendulum must swing to the opposite extreme. That's the nature of energy."

When Colin first moved into Nico's house he was recently divorced and in a vulnerable state. He didn't know that he could have a life like Nico's. They became like brothers and had three-way relationships with many women. He eventually moved away and ended up in Wisconsin, with a job he hated, and a woman he truly loved who took care of him to the end.

As Nico prepared food in the kitchen, he asked from across the room, "Are you still married, Lauren?"

"Of course!"

"What kind of a question is that, Nico?" asked his friend. There was a general stirring of agreement among the guests.

"Well, it's a normal question to ask! I haven't seen Lauren in a long time and people get divorced. That's what they do."

Later on, he asked me two times in a row what my husband's name is, even though he's hung out with him on several occasions. He couldn't remember where we live, though he's been to our home.

A beautiful woman I talked to was shy about mentioning to the others that she was getting married in August. She knew Nico would go off on another anti-marriage diatribe. Nico always says that marriage doesn't work because people change. He hasn't really changed at all. He's stopped drinking and smoking, is financially secure and travels most of the year. He's not as manic as he used to be. Other than that, he is the same.

When Nico was married, he never told his wife about his entire past. He was afraid that she wouldn't accept him for who he was. That is why Nico is now so flamboyantly himself. But he's not as keen to allow others to be themselves. He preaches, and tells people what to do, and tries to break them down. He makes them feel guilty if they do not share all they have with him. If you call for something in return, he's hardly ever there.

Somehow in that awkward transition of figuring out who I was in my early twenties, I went from worshipping Jesus to worshipping Nico. I still wanted a charismatic figure to pin all my dependencies to. I wanted to look up at someone with glistening doe eyes, and always take their word for it. But now I question everything that I am told. I've learned to listen to myself, and trust my ability to reason.

When I initially walked up to Nico's house, the first people I saw were Irving, his wife and two sons. He didn't recognize me at first. I hadn't seen him in five years. He asked me what I was up to, and then brought up the time we wrote a script featuring our cats as the actors re-enacting our relationship. We had called it *Ciao Gatto*.

"I still have the footage somewhere," he said.

"I actually wrote the whole book," I said.

But he didn't quite get what I meant. "Yes we wrote a whole book," he said, still thinking of the script.

At that point, someone interrupted and I didn't get a chance to talk to him again that night. Towards the end of our relationship, I mentioned to Irving that I had begun writing about our relationship. He had said to me then, "You could *never* capture me." All I could think, was, 'Just watch me.'

To Irving and Nico I am just a part of their thousand-piece puzzle. Though in our weird, fucked up way we all love each other, and are perpetually connected by the crazy stories we have shared. I'm certain they think my life is small without them. But what they think doesn't matter to me anymore.

Now I have the benefit of not feeling lost. I can go home to a man who listens and supports, who is strong and secure, who knows that seeing old flames makes me love him even more. Now I am too strong to let anyone hold me down with ropes and guilt, whips and manipulation.

The world is full of people who will try to change you to be more like them. But when you find someone who loves you for exactly who you are, and you feel the same for them; hold on. The best that life has to offer comes when you finally find that.

Epilogue

Today, I find the idea of God to be impossible. Being released from mind-control, guilt, borders, rules, rewards, punishments, and belief in stories that happened thousands of years ago has been enormously freeing for me. I no longer have irrational fears, guilt, or depression because they were constructs of my religious belief.

It makes sense that the faithful think you are fallen when you leave the fold. When I first left the church, I was compelled to experience everything that I had been told was wrong. It appeared as though I just wanted to party rather than pray. Through my exploration, I learned that the world was not at all what I'd been told it was. It was much more complex and beautiful, and I had many lessons to learn to find my own strength.

When I came to understand that there is no God, a tremendous weight lifted off of me. My life was suddenly my own responsibility and no one else's. I became the warrior of my own existence, the hero of my own life, directing its course for an optimum balance of pleasure and productivity. I feel more love than I ever have before. Life after religion is a gift of happiness. I am at peace with the unknown.

Notes

1. Henry Miller, *Tropic of Capricorn* (Grove Press, 1961), 35.

2. Edna St. Vincent Millay, "First Fig," *Edna St. Vincent Millay Selected Poems* (American Poets Project, The Library of America, 2003), 23.

3. Lou Reed, "Perfect Day," *Transformer* (RCA, 1972), Produced by David Bowie and Mick Ronson.

4. Jeanette Winterson, *Sexing The Cherry* (Grove Press, 1989), 140.

5. Colette, *The Pure And The Impure* (New York Review Books, 2000), 173.

6. Depeche Mode, "Enjoy The Silence," *Violator* (Mute, 1990), Written by Martin Gore, Produced by Depeche Mode and Flood.

6. Oscar Wilde, *The Picture of Dorian Gray* (The Modern Library, 1998), 23.

7. Osho, *Maturity – The Responsibility of Being Oneself* (St. Martin's Press, 1999), 12.

8. Norman Mailer, *An American Dream* (Harper Perennial, 2006), 22.

9. Colette, *Claudine At School – The Complete Claudine* (Farrar, Straus and Giroux, 1976), 111.

10. Christopher Hitchens, *God Is Not Great – How Religion Poisons Everything* (Hachette Book Group, 2007), 8.

11. Samuel Johnson, "Anecdotes of the Revd. Percival Stockdale," *Johnsonian Miscellanies* (Oxford Clarendon Press, 1897), vol. II, 333.

12. Jeanette Winterson, *Sexing the Cherry*, 141.

13. Christopher Lasch, *The Culture Of Narcissism* (W.W. Norton & Company, 1979), 338.

14. Christopher Lasch, *The Culture Of Narcissism*, 81.

15. Erica Jong, *Fear of Flying* (Signet, 1974), 137.

23658574R10172

Made in the USA
Charleston, SC
30 October 2013